FAMILIES, INCEST, AND THERAPY

A SPECIAL ISSUE OF
*INTERNATIONAL JOURNAL OF
FAMILY THERAPY*

EDITED BY
CHARLES P. BARNARD, Ed.D.

HUMAN SCIENCES PRESS, INC.
72 FIFTH AVENUE,
NEW YORK, N.Y. 10011

HUMAN SCIENCES PRESS
72 Fifth Avenue
New York, NY 10011

Printed in the United States of America

Library of Congress Catalog Card Number 83-047623
ISBN: 0-89885-126-2
Copyright 1983 by Human Sciences Press

INTERNATIONAL JOURNAL OF

FAMILY THERAPY

CONTENTS

VOLUME 5, NUMBER 2   SUMMER 1983

INTERNATIONAL JOURNAL OF FAMILY THERAPY presents the latest developments in theory, research, and practice with an emphasis on examining the family within the broader socio-economic matrix of which it is an integral part.

MANUSCRIPTS should be submitted to Dr. Gerald Zuk, Editor, INTERNATIONAL JOURNAL OF FAMILY THERAPY, Post Office Box 1697 Johnson Street Station Metairie, Louisiana 70001. Manuscripts should be submitted in triplicate, double-spaced throughout and with a 100 word abstract. Style should conform to the Publication Manual of the American Psychological Association, 2nd Edition (1974). Further information may be obtained from the editor.

INDEXED IN: Multicultural Education Abstracts, Abstracts of Health Care, Biological Abstracts, Management Studies, Current Index to Journals in Education.

SUBSCRIPTIONS are on a calendar year basis: $67 for institutions and $29 for individuals. Prices are slightly higher outside the U.S.

BUSINESS OFFICE: Human Sciences Press, 72 Fifth Avenue, New York, New York,10011.

ADVERTISING inquiries should be made to Human Sciences Press. Rates are available on request.

LC 83-047623   ISSN 0148-8384   IJFTDY 5(2)65-152(1983)

INTRODUCTION

Charles P. Barnard

The contents of this issue are mainly the result of a conference conducted in San Antonio, Texas, April 7 - 8, 1982. The conference was advertised as being designed to "... provide an understanding of incest and suggestions for intervention within a family context." Those in attendance shared the opinion that the goal of the conference was resolutely met. While this writer was listening to the various presentations, and being aware of the concern incestuous families create for clinicians, the notion of a "special issue" of IJFT crystallized. As each of the contributors are certainly deserving of their particular recognition it also seems important to acknowledge the IJFT editor, Dr. Gerald H. Zuk, and Human Sciences Press for their endorsement and support in the development of this project.

The reader, whether novice or experienced clinician, should find the contents a valuable source of information regarding incestuous families. The contributors, most with a rich background in the treatment of incestuous families, provide the reader with a blend of theory, pragmatic treatment considerations, and illustrative clinical vignettes. While incest is regarded as a complex clinical issue this material seems evident to provide greater clarity of understanding and ideas for clinical implementation.

Charles P. Barnard, Ed.D., is Professor and Director, Marriage and Family Therapy, Clinical Services Center, University of Wisconsin-Stout, Menomonie, WI 54751.

International Journal of Family Therapy 5(2), Summer 1983
0148-8384/83/1400-0069$02.75©1983 Human Sciences Press

AN HISTORICAL PERSPECTIVE OF INCEST

Alberto C. Serrano
David W. Gunzburger

ABSTRACT: Incest has been documented in most civilizations and for as long as can be remembered. This article begins with a brief historical overview of incest across cultures and times. The second part includes a review of several theories that place the significance of the incest taboo in an historical continuum.

Despite the fact that incest is a universal preoccupation and despite its documentation in the mythologies and histories of most civilizations, the taboo remains so intense that there is very little open discussion of the subject outside professional circles. It is also interesting to note that, historically, there has been an apparent fluctuation between conservative and liberal attitudes regarding incest both within and between cultures. No single group has been excluded.

Even the exact origins of the word "incest" are unclear. One etymological interpretation holds that the word "incest" derives from the Latin word "castus," meaning pure or chaste, and from "incestus," meaning impure and immodest. However, by the medieval period, "incestus" was defined as immodesty with blood relations or maidens, as well as adultery (Meisch, 1972).

Another interesting interpretation holds the original meaning to derive from the Latin "cestus," meaning girdle of Venus, which

Alberto C. Serrano, M.D., is Clinical Professor of Psychiatry & Pediatrics, and Director of Child & Adolescent Psychiatry, Community Guidance Center, 2135 Babcock Road, San Antonio, TX 78229. David W. Gunzburger, Ph.D., is Psychologist on the Child Abuse Team at the Center. Reprint requests may be sent to Drs. Serrano and Gunzburger at that address.

International Journal of Family Therapy 5(2), summer 1983
0148-8384/83/1400-0070$02.75 © 1983 Human Sciences Press

should arouse love. Losing the girdle was, in Greek tradition, a symbol of sexual activity. According to Homer, the seed of erotic magic charms of Aphrodite, the Goddess of Love, was in the girdle. Nordic sagas too, make reference to the girdle. Here, the stealing of the girdle was a symbol of rape, and the losing of the girdle to any male member of the family other than the husband was an offense against the family sexual taboo (Meisch, 1972).

MYTHOLOGY AND INCEST

Greek mythology is expressive of the incest taboo of that time and culture. Incestuous love among the Gods is a frequent theme. Gaa (Mother Earth) had an incestuous "love embrace" with her son, Uranus, and gave birth to six males and six females, the Titans. One of the Titans, Kronos, knew of his father's/brother's evil deeds, and hated his father as an Oedipal rival. One day, Kronos surprised his brother/father Uranus as he was having marital coitus with Gaa, and castrated him. Kronos seized power and married his sister, Rhea, bearing his three sons and three daughters. His happiness, however, was short lived. His father's fate was repeated. Kronos was unmanned by his son, Zeus, who mastered the throne of the Gods and married his sister, Hera. The children of Zeus,, Minos, and Britomartis, continued the Olympian incest tradition (Meisch. 1972).

As stated above, mythology reveals some of the central themes of the Oedipal complex, the infantile root of the hatred for the father which arises out of the sexual rivalry for the mother. However, in Greek mythology, these incestuous wish impulses were not realized in the mother, but rather were transferred to a sister. Father/daughter incest, while less frequent, is also present in Greek mythology. Perhaps the most famous was the union between Cinyras and Mirrha. Their son, Adonis, was considered the most beautiful of the Demi Gods.

The Bible, too, has two outstanding examples of father/daughter incest. The daughters of Lot, according to the Old Testament, had a liason with their father after the loss of their mother. Salome, in the New Testament, had an incestuous stepfather who was also her uncle. Further, an entire chapter in the Book of Leviticus addressed itself to the integrity of the family life and the rulings concerning the sexual relations of God's people (Henderson, 1972).

While our exact knowledge of the spread of incest in pre-Christian times is sketchy, the mythologies of the Greeks, Roman, Egyptians, and the Persians, which describe frequent incestuous relationships between the Gods, is assumed to have been a reflection of the people's corresponding behaviors. Some of the best documentation comes from ancient Egypt, in which sexual relationships between members of the same family were not only acceptable, but sometimes even required. The most famous marriage of this kind was Cleopatra, who was at the same time her husband's niece and his sister. Incestuous marriages were not just limited to the royal rulers. It appears that such marriages were widespread amongst the Egyptian people in the pre- and post-Christian periods. It is also of interest that in Egyptian poetry, the words brother and sister also have the connotation of both lover and loved, suggestive of the once permitted custom of incestuous marriage (Meisch, 1972). Among the ancient Persians, incestuous marriage was directly recommended. For a period such unions were legally sanctioned for the ruling classes and the priesthood, e.g., it is known that King Cambyses and Emperor Artaxerxes married their own daughters. Among the pre-Columbian Incas, there were marriages between brothers and sisters, which according to the chronicles were part of family law for over fourteen generations. The Hebrews of the pre-Mosaic period allowed marriages between children of the same father, but not of the same mother. Special laws involving punishment for incest took time to develop. For the most part, unions between parent and child were banned, followed by the limiting of unions between brother and sister to half-sisters or half-brothers on the mother's side. However, discontinuities are also noted. The Roman definition of the crime and resultant punishment is reflective of this development.

CHANGING PERCEPTIONS OF INCEST

Historically, there appears to have been a progressive movement away from the acceptance of incestuous relationships. This progression was not continuous either from a legal or social/ethical point of view.

In his annals, Tacitus observed that marriages between cousins of the first degree were unknown in all of Rome and that the bar of marriage reached officially as far as the sixth degree of relationship. This was liberalized to the fourth degree around 200 B.C. Punishment for breaking the law on incest was harsh, and in the early years of the Republic, suicide was enforced. In the first century B.C., punishment included being thrown from the cliff of a mountain in Tarpei. Emperor Constantine and Emperor Theodosius, who made Christianity the state religion in 391, used death by burning and confiscation of property as a punishment. In the sixth century Christian Emperors undertook stiff legal reforms, broadening the ban of marriage between blood relations and sharpening the penalties for incestuous behavior (Meisch, 1972).

One of the most famous cases of incest in Imperial Rome is that of Caligula, who ruled between 37 and 47 of the Christian era. He married his sister, Agrippina, who as the wife of Claudius, also had sexual relations with her son, Nero, by an earlier marriage. Later, during the middle ages and during the progressive Christianization of Europe, the civil law on marriage became increasingly a matter of religious concern. Sexuality was regarded as abhorrent, sinful, and promiscuous, and the incest laws were stretched to include a seventh degree of kinship. Even Godparents and the relatives of a priest who baptized or confirmed the child were banned from marriage to one another. The fear of incest was so deeply rooted that a point was reached when even the two baptismal witnesses of the same child could not marry. Despite these strong regulations, incest continued to be fairly widespread. Apparently, even the clergy were not untouched. Pope John XII, who was deposed in 963, was not only accused of incest with his mother and sisters, but also of having turned the Church of St. John in Lateran into a brothel. Pope Balthasas Cossa, too, confessed before a church council to incest, adultery, and other crimes in 1414 (Meisch, 1972).

Under Innocent III, at the end of the twelfth century, the ban of marriage was liberalized by making it officially permissible for cousins beyond the third degree of relationship to get married. However, agents of the Inquisition, initiated by the same council, frequently employed accusations of homosexual and/or incestuous behavior in the persecution of heretics. During the renaissance, the attitude of the Catholic Church towards sex and incest seemed to become more liberal, although incest was still considered a crime. In 1492, Pope Alexander VI, involved his daughter in a notorious scandal. In a papal bull, he announced himself the father of one of his daughter's children and through a second bull, ascribed fatherhood to his son. Other condotieri, and even another pope, Pope John XXII, were a part of documented cases of incest.

Religious changes brought by reformation and counter reformation reinforced the notions of the sanctity of marriage. The punishment for the "sin" of incest again became heavier. Anne Boleyn, beheaded by Henry VIII, was accused not only of adultery, but also of incest with her brother. It was her daugher, Queen Elizabeth, who empowered the high court to appeal the death penalty to incest and to introduce fines and imprisonment for the crime. The ruling class, however, continued to circumvent the law and it was said that Cardinal Richelieu had an incestuous relationship with Madam Rousse, his illegitimate daughter.

Despite a well-documented history of incestuous cases, Murdock (1969) examined 250 societies in a cross-cultural study and concluded that there is no group which allows incest within the immediate circle of the family (between mother and son, father and daughter, or between brothers and sisters) with the exceptions of Egypt, Peru, and Hawaii (Meisch, 1972). The anthropologist Levi-Strauss includes Asande, Madagascar, and Burma in this list of exceptions. Levi-Strauss emphasizes, however, that these are exceptions, and within this list, incest is typically either a privilege of the narrow social cast, or ritualistic in character (Levi-Strauss, 1969). For example, parent/child masturbation has been observed among certain tribes and cultures who have an official ban on incest. Masturbatory handling of the children by their parents belongs to an ancient tradition and is still practiced today amongst, for example, the Arabs, Moslems, and the Islamic population of Central Asia. The North American Hopi frequently masturbate their children. The motives for this behavior are varied, and most often connected with superstitious attitudes (to encourage the growth of the genitals or to develop and assure vaginal sexuality). Such masturbation is also used in some cultures to keep the child quiet. Interestingly, neither guilt nor psychological harm of the children appears to result.

On the other hand, the North American Mojave Indians forbid masturbation of their infants and small children in that they believe this would make them "think of incest." The tribe lives under an exceptionally strict incest taboo which forbids marriage even to second cousins. The Mojave Indians connect incest to witchcraft and see it as an evil sign forecasting the destruction of the family. Their etiology also links incest very closely with suicide. Other North American Indian tribes fear the birth of a child conceived in incest as reflective of a catastrophe which might affect all members of the tribe. The fear is so great, that the pregnancy is terminated immediately. The Navajo are an example in that they regard abortion as an absolute need in incestuous pregnancies.

ROOTS OF THE INCEST TABOO

To understand the development and significance of the incest taboo we turn first to Freud. Freud offers a psychological basis for incest prohibitions. In *Totem and Taboo* (1953) he proposed, similarly to Darwin, that early humans lived in a hoard controlled by violent, tyrannical fathers who kept all the females for themselves and drove away their sons to prevent competition. Freud suggested that the mistreated sons eventually joined forces, overwhelmed the father, and ate him in a cannibalistic victory celebration. However, their jubilation was short lived. Remorse, deriving from admiration for their father resulted, and with remorse came the realization that their plan of gaining sexual access to their father's women would create savage competition among themselves and destroy the power that they found in unity. Therefore, they joined together in renouncing the sexual claim on the women by creating the incest taboo and concomitant rules of exogamy. Freud (1953) believed that the ban on incest became the basis of society and morality, and hence, the beginnings of cultural development. Although the primeval story has never gained wide acceptance, Freud's original insight constitutes a most important contribution to the field.

Another theory has been advanced by the anthropologist, Malinowsky (1927), who stated that intrafamilial sex, except between marriage partners, was taboo because it would have been extremely disruptive to family relationships. He stated that incest would mean the upsetting of age distinctions, a mixing of generations, the disorganization of sentiment, and a violent exchange of roles at a time when the family is a most important educational medium. He contended that no society could exist under such conditions and that basically, mating with the parent would involve courtship behavior that would interfere with the adequate development of the young.

Levi-Strauss (1969) stated that kinship terms and systems tell people whom to marry and whom not to marry. He contends that we are all born into a society, and universally, society's most pressing issue is the exchange of everything imaginable. The basic irreducible exchange is the exchange of women in marriages. Marriage rules are always destined to establish a system of exchange. The prohibition of incest is a rule of reciprocity. A woman "whom one does not take and one whom one may not take is for that very reason offered up" (Levi-Strauss, 1969). Levi-Strauss (1969) held that the transition from nature to culture is determined by man's ability to think of kinship relationships as systems of oppositions; oppositions between the men who own and the women who are owned, between wives who are acquired and sisters and daughters who are given away; and opposition between two types of bonds, bonds of alliance, and bonds of kinship. From this perspective, that which we traditionally call incest prohibition is more simply a focused expression of a more general set of regulations and oppositions. Hence, exceptions such as those found in Egypt, Peru, and Hawaii are not exceptions at all, and seem so only from the view-point of other societies with stricter incest prohibitions. Every society regulates marriageability. There is no society in which every possible union is sanctioned. The incest taboo, which generally prohibits mating among members of the nuclear family is in fact not aimed at the family. The taboo is rather a means of guaranteeing the exchange of women (Levi-Strauss, 1969).

Levi-Strauss continues that if the incest taboo is in one shape or another universal, then society is confronted with a group of facts not far from scandal, that is, a universal rule combines the characteritics of two mutually exclusive orders, nature and culture; nature, the domain of universality, and culture, the domain of rules. This "scandal" is clarified by Lindsey (1967). He points to the biologically guaranteed maladaptive consequences that stem from brother/sister and parent/child breeding. The essential question then becomes whether or not there is evidence for the existence of a strong and pervasive incestuous impulse that would be interfered with by such a taboo. Widespread incest in our society is held as evidence for such impulses.

Statistics from Kinsey (1953), Gebhardt (1965), and others suggest an incidence of incest of about two cases per thousand population. More recently, however, it has been proposed that these figures represent a substantial understatement and that one percent is possibly a more realistic figure (Meiselman, 1964; Finkelhor, 1978). It seems as if one is given completely free choice, a wholly biologic choice, people would mate with those closest. In other words, a man is a compromised being, jeopardized and conflicted at his essence by impulses propelling him towards incest and a hereditary outcome that militates against it.

We have been led to pose the problem of incest in connection with the relationship between man's biological existence and his social existence and we have immediately established that the prohibition could not be ascribed accurately to either one or the other. This union is neither static nor arbitrary and as soon as it comes into being, the whole situation is completely changed. Indeed, it is less a union than a transformation. Before, it, culture is still nonexistent; with it, nature's sovereignty over man is ended. The prohibition of incest is where nature transcends itself. It sparks the formation of a new and more complex type of structure and is superimposed under the simpler structures of physical life through integration, just as these themselves are superimposed upon the simple structures of animal life. It brings about, and is in itself, the advent of a new order. Considered as a prohibition, the prohibition of incest merely affirms in a field vital to the group survival, the preeminence of the social order over the natural, the collective over the individual, organization over the arbitrary (Levi-Strauss, 1969).

The point that Levi-Strauss makes is that sexual regulations are not independent systems, but aspects of systems of exchange. Incest taboos, that is, sexual regulations, are the most focused part of systems of exchange because a woman is not simply a woman, but someone's daughter, sister or mother. To give or receive a daughter, sister or mother, is to transform one or all of these into a wife. Woman, daughter, sister and mother are biological facts. Wife is a social fact. Thus, it is that marriage transforms the biological into the social.

While Levi-Strauss has offered a social basis for the incest taboo and Lindsey a biological basis, Freud has offered a psychological basis for incest prohibitions. Freud was impressed with the large number of female patients who reported being abused sexually by their fathers and brothers. He suggested that at the source of adult psychological problems one could find childhood sexual traumatic experiences. He then developed the notion that it was not the childhood experience, but the failure to resolve the Oedipal situation and to give up the fantasies and transfer the impulses to more socially acceptable objects that was the source of such problems.

Why Freud changed his mind has been the source of recent speculation. Perhaps he was afraid of confronting his peers, colleagues, friends, and even his own father. What is clear, however, is that the focus was shifted from the victimizer/offender and a change in theoretical structure placed the responsibility on the victim.

As does Freud, Schechner (1971) analyzes the plays of Oedipus and Hamlet in the context of the love of a son for his mother. The interpretation of these works, however, could be quite different, that is, in terms of a love of the mother for her son. In Oedipus, Jocasta hears that Laius has ordered the death of her infant, Oedipus. She cannot bring herself to murder her son, so she cruelly binds his feet and gives him over to the shepherd to be abandoned to the weather. The shepherd pities the infant and gives him to another shepherd who works for the King of Corinth. The boy is raised in Corinth and when he is grown, he hears of the Oracle, and flees to escape his doom; he is to kill his father. In flight, he meets Laius on a road and slays him. Later, Oedipus solves the riddle of the sphinx that was terrorizing the city of Thebes. He is received as a hero, becomes a king, and is offered the hand of Queen Jocasta. Is Jocasta unaware of the similarity in names between her former husband (i.e., Laius or lame) and her new husband (i.e., Oedipus or swollen feet)? Is she unaware of the unique scars so characteristic as to give Oedipus his name? Is she unaware that Oedipus' age is that of her abandoned son? Does she not mention in the play that Oedipus looks very much like Laius? Jocasta bore Laius no more children after Oedipus, but she quickly bears Oedipus four children. On that fateful day, when the events of the past come to light, Oedipus is particularly agitated that the old shepherd admits that it was Jocasta who gave Laius' child over. It would be difficult to deny Freud's insight that children wish to murder their parents. But what of the parents (Schechner, 1971)?

It is not unlikely that Jocasta had her incestuous wishes, that these wishes run in all directions; however, it would be hard to defend the notion that "Jocasta's complex" has an independent existence. Schechner (1971) suggests that there are two facets to an incestuous wish relationship, just as there are two partners to

ALBERTO C. SERRANO, DAVID W. GUNZBURGER

sexual intercourse. It is not fair to emphasize the role of the child and ignore that of the parent. We must note that it is members of the parent generation who write about incestuous wishes. It is not surprising then that children are emphasized. Thus, the fault that Lindsey (1967) describes runs in several directions, both within and between generations. There are two incest crises in life, the child's crisis, with secondary repercussions in the parents, occurring when the child wants what is forbidden: his or her parents or siblings as a mate, and the parent's crisis, with secondary repercussions for the child, occurring when the parent wants what is forbidden: his or her child as a mate, and is typically resolved, by "marrying off" the child. Incestuous wishes then, probably affect every person throughout life. The adolescent crisis is often as disorienting for the sexually aroused parent as it is for the sexually aroused child. The need for an active solution is implied by Levi-Strauss. He states that the prohibition of the sexual use of a daughter or sister compels one to give a daughter or sister in marriage to another man and at the same time, establishes a right to the daughter or sister of this other man. Thus, the problem is resolved by transforming the incestuous impulse into a socially sanctioned marriage exchange (Levi-Straus, 1969).

Murdock (1969) proposed that an adequate explanation for the incest taboo required a multidisciplinary approach utilizing ideas drawn from psychoanalysis, sociology, behavioristic psychology, and cultural anthropology. Freud's theory of the universally repressed desire for incestuous relationships could account for the intensity of the incest horror through the ego defense mechanism of reaction formation. It often results in the strong condemnation of others for ideas or behaviors that one is struggling to keep repressed in oneself. On a sociological level, the incest taboo would serve the function of preventing sexual competition and jealousy within the family. Furthermore, the taboo would serve an important function of allowing society's families to adequately achieve their primary role of acculturation of children.

Finkelhor (1978) reports that nearly one in five girls and one in eleven boys have had a sexual experience as a child with an older person. The experiences cut across social class and ethnic lines. He reports that sexual victimization of children has not increased in the past 30 years. There has, however, been an historical evolution as outlined above. Attempts to resolve the problem of incest have been made on the social plane. On the individual plane, there appears to be no complete resolution and too often, the transformation from nature to culture fails to succeed and incest impulses are acted upon. At times the victim has been the focus, at other times the victimizer. In our present society, however, this dichotomy appears false. It is held that the historical evolution outlined above is continuing. The view of the sexual abusing/incestuous family as a dysfunctional system, would be the most productive unit of analysis for successful resolution.

REFERENCES

Finkelhor, D. Psychological, cultural, and family factors in incest and family sexual abuse. *Journal of Marriage and Family Counseling.* 1978, *4*, 41–50.

Freud, S. Totem and taboo. *Obras Completes.* Buenos Aires: Santiago Rueda, 1953.

Gebhardt, P. Sex offenders: An analysis of types. New York: Harper and Row, 1965.

Henderson, D.J. Incest: A synthesis of data. *Canadian Psychiatric Association Journal*, 1972, *17*, 299–312.

Kinsey, A. Sexual behavior in the human female. Philadelphia: U.B. Saunders, 1953.

Levi-Strauss, C. The elementary structures of kinship. Boston: Beacon press, 1969.

Lindsey, G. Some remarks concerning incest, "The incest taboo and psychoanalytic theory". *American Psychologist*, 1967, *22*, 1050–1059.

Malinowsky, B. Sex and repression in savage society. London: Routledge, Kogan, Paul, 1927.

Meisch, H. Incest. London: Andre Deutsch Limited Publishers, 1972.

Meiselman, K. Incest. San Francisco: Josey-Bass Publishers, 1964.

Murdock, G.P. Social Structure. New York: Macmillan, 1969.

Schechner, R. Incest and culture: A reflexion on Claude Levi-Strauss. *The Psychoanalytic Review*, 1971, *58*, 563–572.

Recognition and Treatment
of Incestuous Families

Judith Herman

ABSTRACT: Incest is a major mental health problem, in terms of both prevalence and morbidity. Father-daughter incest constitutes the majority of reported cases. The possibility of incest should be considered in a family which includes a violent father, a disabled mother, a child in an adult maternal role, or an "acting out" adolescent girl. Intervention requires recognition of the criminal and addictive aspects of the father's behavior. Active cooperation between mental health professionals and mandated child protective and law enforcement agencies is necessary for effective treatment. Group therapy and affiliated self-help programs appear to be the treatment modality of choice. Rehabilitation of the family is based upon restoration of the mother-daughter bond as a guarantee of safety for the child.

THE PROBLEM OF INCEST

Incest, the sexual abuse of children within their families, is a major mental health problem which until recently has gone largely unrecognized within the mental health professions. Several large-scale surveys of predominantly white, middle-class populations have consistently documented the fact that about 10 percent of all women report a childhood sexual experience with an older male relative, and at least 1 percent of all women have had a sexual experience with a father or stepfather (Kinsey 1953; Landis, 1956; Finkelhor, 1979). The risk to boys is not as well documented, but some clinicians believe that cases involving male victims may be

Judith Herman, M.D., is Assistant Clinical Professor, Psychiatry, at the Cambridge Hospital, Harvard Medical School. Reprint requests may be sent to Dr. Herman at 61 Roseland Street, Somerville, MA 02143.

International Journal of Family Therapy 5(2), Summer 1983
0148-8384/83/1400-0081$02.75©1983 Human Sciences Press

significantly underreported (Dixon, 1978). When boys are molested within their families, the abuser is as likely to be a father as a mother (Maisch, 1972; Meiselman, 1978; Justice, 1979).

Incestuous abuse usually begins when the child is between the ages of six and 12, though cases involving younger children, including infants, have been reported. The sexual contact typically begins with fondling and gradually proceeds to masturbation and oralgenital contact. Vaginal intercourse is not usually attempted, at least until the child reaches puberty. Physical violence is not often employed, since the overwhelming authority of the parent is usually sufficient to gain the child's compliance. The sexual contact becomes a compulsive behavior for the father, whose need to preserve sexual access to his daughter becomes the organizing principle of family life. The sexual contact is usually repeated in secrecy for years, ending only when the child finds the resources to escape. The child victim keeps the secret, fearing that if she tells she will not be believed, she will be punished, or she will destroy the family (Summit, 1982).

Incestuously abused children exhibit a wide variety of distress symptoms including nightmares, bedwetting, fearfulness, social withdrawal or misbehavior, and somatic complaints, particularly lower abdominal or pelvic pain (Brandt, 1977; Burgess, 1978a; Sgroi, 1978). Symptoms in adolescence include runaway attempts, suicide attempts, drug and alcohol abuse, hysterical seizures, indiscriminate sexual activity, and early pregnancy (Herman, 1981; Goodwin 1982). The destructive effects of the incest appear to persist into adult life, long after the sexual contact has ended. Adult women with a history of incest have persistent and often severe impairments in self-esteem, intimate relationships, and sexual functioning (Meiselman, 1978; Herman, 1981). Incest victims also apparently run a higher than normal risk for repeated victimization (battering and rape) (Herman, 1981). Marriage to an abusive spouse, with potential repetition of the abuse in the next generation, is a frequent outcome (Goodwin, 1982).

RECOGNIZING THE INCESTUOUS FAMILY

Incest occurs in all social classes, racial and ethnic groups. The vast majority of cases, probably over 90 percent, never come to the attention of any social agency (Gagnon, 1965). Poor and disorganized families are heavily overrepresented among reported cases because they lack the resources to preserve secrecy.

Incestuous families are not easily recognizable because of their conventional appearance. In most cases, the family structure represents a pathological exaggeration of generally accepted patriarchal norms. Incestuous fathers are often well-respected in their communities. They are frequently described as "good providers," and their wives are often completely dependent upon them for economic survival. Incestuous fathers often attempt to isolate their families, restricting both the mobility and the social contacts of their wives and daughters. It is not unusual for the daughters to report that their mothers cannot drive a car, that the family never has visitors, or that they are not allowed to participate in normal peer activities because of their fathers' jealousy and suspiciousness. Finally, incestuous fathers often enforce their dominance in the family through violence. In a survey of 40 women with an incest history, over half reported having witnessed their fathers beating their mothers or other children (Herman, 1981). The daughters singled out for the sexual relationship is usually spared the beatings; however, she understands clearly what might happen to her if she incurs her father's displeasure.

For these reasons, incestuous fathers are often described as "family tyrants" (Weinberg, 1955; Cormier, 1962; Maisch, 1972). However, once the incest has been detected, they are unlikely to present in this manner in a clinical interview. On the contrary, they commonly appear as pathetic, meek, bewildered, and ingratiating (Walters, 1975). Because they are exquisitely sensitive to the realities of power, they rarely attempt to intimidate anyone who has equal or greater social status, such as an adult professional. Rather, they will attempt to gain the professional's sympathy and seek to deny, minimize, or rationalize their abusive behavior. Inexperienced professionals may incorrectly conclude that the father is a relatively powerless figure in the family and may even describe the family system as mother-dominated.

Most mothers in incestuous families, however, are not in any position to dominate their husbands; often they can barely take care of themselves and their children. One of the most consistent findings in the literature is the unusually high rate of serious illness or disability in mothers of sexually abused daughters (Maisch, 1972; Browning, 1977; Finkelhor, 1979; Herman, 1981). Undiagnosed major mental illness: schizophrenia, depression, or alcoholism, is frequently observed in the mothers.

It should be noted also that one of the most common cause of maternal "disability" in the incestuous family is the mother' inability to take control of her reproductive life. Numerous survey have documented the fact that incestuous families have mor children than the prevailing norms (Tormes, 1968; Lukianowicz 1972; Maisch, 1972; Herman, 1981).

Economically dependent, socially isolated, battered, ill, o encumbered with the care of many small children, mothers in incestuous families are generally not in a position to conside independent survival, and must therefore preserve their marriages at all costs, even if the cost includes the conscious or unconscious sacrifice of a daughter.

Incestuous fathers do not assume maternal caretaking functions when their wives are disabled; rather, they expect to continue to receive female nurturance. The oldest daughter is usually deputized to take on a "little mother" role, often assuming major responsibility for housework and child care (Kaufman, 1954; Lustig, 1966; Justice, 1979; Herman, 1981). The daughter's sexual relationship with the father often evolves as an extension of her other duties. As the oldest daughter reaches adolescence and becomes more resistant, the father may turn his attention sequentially to the younger daughters. Repetition of the incest with more than one daughter or with other available children (nieces, stepchildren, grandchildren) has been a common finding of numerous reports (Cavallin, 1966; Herman, 1981).

Sexual estrangement of the marital couple is frequently cited as a factor in the genesis of incest. However, careful interviewing of offenders and their wives indicates that most incestuous fathers continue to have sex on demand with their wives as well as their daughters; those fathers who confine their sexual activities to their children do so by choice (Groth, 1979). Similarly, alcoholism, though frequently observed in the fathers, does not seem to play a determining role in the development of overt incest; problem drinking is reported as frequently in fathers who are seductive but not overtly incestuous, and in the general population (Herman, 1981). To be sure, many fathers attempt to excuse their behavior by attributing it to "demon alcohol"; however, careful interviewing again reveals that the compelling sexual fantasy is present when the father is sober. He may drink in order to provide a "time out" during which he can disclaim responsibility for his actions (Groth, 1979).

To summarize the known risk factors: father-daughter incest should be suspected in any family which includes a violent or domineering and suspicious father; a battered, chronically ill or disabled mother; or a daughter who appears to have assumed major adult responsibilities. Though the oldest daughter is particularly vulnerable, once incest has been reported with one child, all other children to whom the father has intimate access should be considered at risk. Incest should also be suspected as a precipitant in the behavior of adolescent girls who present as runaways, delinquents, or with drug abuse or suicide attempts.

In situations where these risk factors are present, questions about incest should be incorporated into the initial interview. Indeed, given the known prevalence of incest, a case can be made for including questions about sexual contacts between adults and children routinely in all evaluations. The main obstacle to obtaining a history of incest is the clinician's reluctance to ask about it. Incest provokes strong emotional reactions even among seasoned professionals. Denial, avoidance, and distancing are universal responses. Clinicians may have particular difficulty considering the possibility of incest in families of similar racial, ethnic, religious, or class backgrounds to their own, while families that are comfortably different may be more easily suspected.

For a clinician who has mastered these countertransference reactions, obtaining a history does not present unusual difficulties. Calm, direct questioning is often sufficient. For children, some specialized interviewing techniques have been developed; these include the use of drawings and anatomically correct dolls (Burgess, 1978b; Goodwin, 1982; Adams-Tucker, 1982). Using these materials, even very young children are able to describe what has happened to them and to distinguish fantasy from reality. False complaints of sexual abuse are rare; on the other hand, it is common for a child to retract a true allegation under pressure from the family (Goodwin, 1982).

CRISIS INTERVENTION

The discovery of incest represents a major family crisis, requiring rapid and decisive intervention. Usually, by the time of the disclosure, the incest has been going on for several years, and the family's defenses have been organized around preservation of the incest secret. Disclosure represents a serious disruption to established patterns of functioning and a threat to the survival of the family. The father faces loss of the sexual activity which has become an addiction. He also faces possible loss of his wife and family, social stigmatization, and even criminal sanctions, though in practice these are virtually never applied. The mother faces possible loss of her husband, social stigmatization, and the terrifying prospect of raising her family alone, a task for which she is ill prepared.

In this situation, the father usually reacts by maintaining steadfast denial. He insists that the child is lying and directs his efforts to persuading his wife and outsiders that he is innocent. The mother finds herself torn between her husband and her daughter. Though she may initially believe the child and attempt to take protective action, unless she receives rapid and effective support she will usually rally to her husband's side within a week or two. If she persists in believing her child, she has a great deal to lose and very little to gain. The daughter, therefore, may find herself discredited, shamed, punished for bringing trouble on the family, and still unprotected from continued sexual abuse. Suicide and runaway attempts are particularly likely at this time. Without effective intervention, the child may be scapegoated and driven out of the family.

Unfortunately, most therapists are not well prepared to intervene in this crisis, because they fail to recognize incest either as criminal or as addictive behavior. This can be seen most commonly in the resistance to the use of criminal terms, "offender" and "victim," and in the failure to report incest to child protective agencies, even though such reporting is mandated by law. Naive therapists may tend to accept the offender's denial or his assurances that the sexual abuse has stopped. Therapists may also be seduced by the offender's rationalizations, all of which are widely supported in popular and professional culture. The most common rationalizations are first, that incest is harmless, or would be if not for prudish social condemnation; second that incest is consensual, and that children are willing participants; and third, that incest is simply a response to deprivation of adult sexual expression and can be treated as such.

Failing to recognize the criminal and addictive nature of the abusive behavior, the therapist may approach the family as though incest were merely a symptom of family dysfunction. He may attempt to treat the underlying dynamics, using a traditional individual or family therapy model in which the therapy contract is freely chosen, one therapist assumes full treatment responsibility, and the rule of confidentiality is observed. This model, which is useful and appropriate for neurotic and some psychotic patients, is ineffective for addicts and for character-disordered patients who commit crimes. Successful crisis intervention with incestuous families requires an active, directive, even coercive approach, and it requires ongoing cooperation between the therapist and agencies of the state: law enforcement and child protective services. No therapist can treat incest alone (Summit, 1981).

Because the problem of incest has only recently claimed the serious attention of mental health professionals, principles and techniques of therapeutic intervention are still in the early stages of development. Successful intervention with the incestuous family clearly requires a high degree of institutional coordination, clinical sophistication, and plain hard work. Well-documented treatment outcome studies do not as yet exist, and even published program descriptions are rare. The following treatment guidelines are derived from site visits to five of the most fully developed treatment programs in different areas of the country, and from verbal reports of clinicians working in 40 to 50 other programs. They represent an attempt to define points of consensus and of controversy among experienced clinicians in the field. A fuller elaboration of these guidelines may be found elsewhere (Herman, 1981).

The initial focus of crisis intervention should be on stopping the sexual abuse and establishing a safe environment in the family. Reporting to the mandated authorities should be done promptly, preferably in the presence of the family, and should be explained as a protective, nonpunitive measure. The therapist must assume that the child's complaint of sexual abuse is valid and should not be confused by initial denial on the part of the parents.

Once the incest has been reported, debate often revolves around whether or not the child should be temporarily removed from the home. In some cases this appears to be the only practical means of ensuring the child's safety. However, this intervention is destructive to the child for several reasons. First, it makes her feel that she has done something wrong and is being punished by banishment from her family; second, it reinforces the tendency of the parental couple to bond against the child; and third, it is difficult to find an appropriate placement for the child. If safety cannot be guaranteed at home, it is much preferable to have the father leave during the crisis period. Unfortunately, child protective agencies do not have the legal authority to remove a parent from the home; however, this result can often be accomplished either by persuasion or in some states through the use of civil protection laws. A court order may be obtained requiring the father to vacate the home and to provide child support for a limited time. Conditions for supervised visitation and for mandated treatment may also be established by the court. Clinicians working with incestuous families should become familiar with these legal procedures.

During the crisis period, all family members are in need of intensive support. The child needs to be assured that there are protective adults outside her family who believe her story and will not allow her to be further exploited. She should be praised for her courage in revealing the incest secret, assured that she is not to blame for the incest, and told that she is helping, not hurting her family by seeking outside help. She should also be told explicitly that many children retract their initial complaints, and that she will not be abandoned should this happen in her case. The mother needs help believing her daughter and resisting the tendency to bond with her husband against the child. If the couple separates, the mother also needs help with issues of practical survival. Previously untreated health problems should also receive prompt attention. The father needs help facing the fact that secrecy has been irrevocably broken, and that he must now admit and give up the sexual relationship with his daughter before the family can be restored.

The crisis initiated by the revelation of the incest secret is resolved at the point that the family is under the supervision of the mandated agency and a coordinated treatment plan is in place. Cooperation between all professionals working with the family facilitates quick and effective crisis intervention and greatly improves the prospects for treatment.

TREATMENT IN THE POST-CRISIS PERIOD

Following the crisis of disclosure, the incestuous family is generally so divided and fragmented that family treatment is not the modality of choice. Experienced practitioners who have begun programs with a family therapy orientation have almost uniformly abandoned this modality except in late stages of treatment (Giarretto, 1978; Summit, 1981). Group treatment for mothers, fathers, and child victims appears to be a far more promising approach. In some cases, individual, couple, or family therapy may be recommended in addition to group. For all family members, the issues of stigmatization, isolation, and poor self-esteem are especially amenable to group treatment. For fathers, group treatment is effective also in breaking through denial and rationalization of the criminal behavior. Many group programs for offenders follow a highly structured model similar to programs for the treatment of alcoholism and other addictions. In early stages of treatment, the offender acknowledges that he has lost control of his behavior and must submit to external control. Progression through the program involves increasing acceptance of responsibility for present behavior and restitution to others for past abuses (Silver, 1976; Brecher, 1978).

Opinion is divided on whether incest offenders can be motivated to remain in treatment without a credible threat of criminal sanctions for failure to comply. To date, the most highly developed treatment programs for incest have been those which rely on a court mandate (Giarretto, 1978; Berliner, 1981). No program has yet demonstrated an ability to engage offenders in sustained treatment without legal sanctions.

In addition to group and individual treatment, many programs incorporate a partial self-help component, most frequently called Parents United and Daughters and Sons United. Self-help activities supplement more formal therapeutic work in a number of ways. During the crisis period, the family's intense need for support may be met by frequent peer contact. The father in particular may be more easily persuaded to admit the incest and cooperate with a treatment program if he is rapidly put in contact with other offenders who have successfully participated in treatment. In the post-crisis period, families beginning treatment may benefit from the experience of those further along, while "advanced" group members may gain self-esteem from being in a helping role. Finally, after formal treatment is terminated, self-help groups provide a continued source of support and community.

CRITERIA FOR TERMINATING TREATMENT

Restoration of the incestuous family centers on the mother-daughter relationship. On this point, there seems to be wide consensus among experienced practitioners, even those most committed to reuniting the parental couple (Giarretto, 1978). Safety for the child is not established simply by improving the sexual or marital relationship of the parents; it is established only when the mother feels strong enough to protect herself and her children, and when the daughter feels sure that she can turn to her mother for protection.

The father may be judged ready to return to his family when he has admitted and taken full responsibility for the incest, apologized to his daughters in the presence of all family members, and promised never to abuse his children again. When the father is ready to return to the family, the family may or may not be ready and willing to receive him. This choice properly rests with the mother, once the mother-daughter bond has been restored, and once neither mother nor daughter feels intimidated. A decision for divorce may be as valid as a decision to rebuild the marriage; certainly the preservation of the parents' marriage should not be considered the criterion of therapeutic success. Probably the best gauge of successful treatment is the child victim's subjective feeling of safety and well-being, the disappearance of her distress symptoms, and the resumption of her interrupted normal development.

Given the present state of therapeutic knowledge, no one can claim to "cure" incest; rather, the behavior may be brought under control, first by outside intervention, second by empowering the mother as a protective agent within the family system, and finally to a limited degree by developing the father's inner controls. The father's internal controls should never be considered sufficient to ensure safety for the child; if the family decides to reunite, mother and daughter should be explicitly prepared for an attempt to resume the incestuous relationship (Groth, 1979). Some degree of outside supervision should probably be maintained as long as children remain in the home.

Further investigation is needed in order to continue the development of effective treatment for all family members. Direct clinical studies of incestuous fathers are still quite rare and largely confined to convicted offenders, who comprise a very small and skewed sample. Long-term follow-up studies of treated and untreated families, and comparative studies of differing treatment approaches are needed in order to document what is at present part of the oral culture of recent clinical experience.

REFERENCES

Adams-Tucker, C. Early treatment of child incest victims. Paper presented at the Annual Meeting of the American Psychiatric Association, Toronto, Canada, 1982.

Berliner, L. King's county approach to sexual abuse. In Bulkley, J. (Ed.), *Innovations in the prosecution of child sexual abuse cases.* Washington, D.C.: American Bar Asociation, 1981.

Brandt, R., & Tisza, V. The sexually misused child. *American Journal of Orthopsychiatry,* 1977, *47*, 80–90.

Brecher, E. *Treatment programs for sex offenders.* Washington, D.C.: U.S. Government Printing Office, 1978.

Browning, D., & Boatman, B. Incest: Children at risk. *American Journal of Psychiatry,* 1977, *134*, 69–72.

Burgess, A., & Holmstrom, L. Accessory-to-sex: Pressure, sex, and secrecy. In Burgess, A. et al. (Eds.), *Sexual assault of children and adolescents.* Lexington, MA: D. C. Heath, 1978.

Burgess, A., & Holmstrom, L. Interviewing young victims. In Burgess, A. et al., *Sexual assault of children,* 1978.

Cavallin, H. Incestuous fathers: A clinical report. *American Journal of Psychiatry,* 1966, *122,* 1132–1138.

Cormier, B., Kennedy, M., & Sangowicz, J. Psychodynamics of father-daughter incest. *Canadian Psychiatric Association Journal,* 1962, *7,* 203–215.

Dixon, K., Arnold, E., & Calestro, K. Father-son incest: Underreported psychiatric problem? *American Journal of Psychiatry,* 1978, *135,* 835–838.

Finkelhor, D. *Sexually victimized children.* New York: Free Press, 1979.

Gagnon, J. Female child victims of sex offenses. *Social Problems,* 1965, *13,* 176–192.

Giarretto, H., Giarretto, A., & Sgroi, S. Coordinated community treatment of incest. In Burgess, A. et al. (Eds.), *Sexual assault of children,* 1978.

Goodwin, J. *Sexual abuse: Incest victims and their families.* Boston, Mass.: John Wright, 1982.

Groth, N. *Men who rape: The psychology of the offender.* New York: Plenum, 1979.

Herman, J. *Father-daughter incest.* Cambridge, Mass.: Harvard University Press, 1981.

Justice, B., & Justice, R. *The broken taboo.* New York: Human Sciences Press, 1979.

Kaufman, I., Peck, A., & Tagiuri, C. The family constellation and overt incestuous relations between father and daughter. *American Journal of Orthopsychiatry,* 1954, *24,* 266–279.

Kinsey, A.C. et al. *Sexual behavior in the human female.* Philadelphia, PA: Saunders, 1953.

Landis, J. Experiences of 500 children with adult sexual deviation. *Psychiatric Quarterly Supplement,* 1956, *30,* 91–109.

Lukianowicz, N. Incest. *British Journal of Psychiatry,* 1972, *120,* 301–313.

Lustig, N. Dresser, J., Murrary, T., & Spellman, S. Incest. *Archives of General Psychiatry,* 1966, *14,* 31–40.

Maisch, H. *Incest.* New York: Stein & Day, 1972.

Meiselman, K. *Incest.* San Francisco: Jossey-Bass, 1978.

Sgroi, S. Child sexual assault: Some guidelines for intervention and assessment. In A. Burgess et al. (Eds.), *Sexual assault of children,* 1978.

Silver, S. Outpatient treatment for sexual offenders. *Social Work,* 1976, 134–140.

Summit, R. Sexual child abuse, the psychotherapist, and the team concept. In *Dealing with child sexual abuse.* Chicago, IL: National Committee for Prevention of Child Abuse, 1981.

Summit, R. Beyond belief: The reluctant discovery of incest. In M. Kirkpatrick (Ed.), *Women's sexual experience.* New York: Plenum, 1982.

Tormes, Y. *Child victims of incest.* Denver, CO: American Humane Association, 1968.

Walters, D. *Physical and sexual abuse of children.* Bloomington, IN: Indiana University, Press, 1975.

Weinberg, S. *Incest behavior.* New York: Citadel, 1955.

Counseling the Incest Offender

Carol Fowler
Susan R. Burns
Janet E. Roehl

ABSTRACT: The Center Against Sexual Assault in Phoenix, Arizona is currently treating 50 incest offenders in its Offender Group treatment program. The average age range is 31 – 45 years old, and 80 percent were sexually or physically abused as children. These men have been found to be extremely self-centered, exhibit poor impulse control, and possess a strong denial of reality. The treatment program includes several intake sessions to ascertain suitability of the offender to this type of therapeutic approach and a stated self-admission of at least the possibility of incestuous involvement. The offenders work in groups, as well as individual sessions.

What is incest? Incest is the sexual abuse of a minor by either an adult related to the child by blood or marriage, or by an adult living within the family and perceived by the child as a member of the family.

Who is the incest offender, the person who sexually uses and abuses his own child? Of the 50 offenders seen for long-term therapy at the Center Against Sexual Assault (CASA), all are males. Eighty percent are between the ages of 31 – 45, with two of the 50 being under 20 years of age and only one over 60 years old. Ninety percent have at least a high school education, and the median income is $20,000 a year. Eighty percent of the offenders were sex-

Carol Fowler, M.A., M.C., is Associate Director at the Center Against Sexual Assault, 1131 East Missouri, Phoenix, AZ 85014. Susan R. Burns is President, Board of Directors at the Center. Janet E. Roehl, Ph.D., is the Division of Continuing Education at the University of Wisconsin-Stout, Menomonie, WI 54751. Reprints requests may be sent to Ms. Fowler.

International Journal of Family Therapy 5(2), Summer 1983
0148-8384/83/1400-0092$02.75©1983 Human Sciences Press

ually or physically mistreated as children, and 67 percent are substance abusers as adults. The ethnic breakdown is 72 percent white, 20 percent Mexican American, 4 percent black, and 4 percent Native American.

CHARACTERISTICS OF OFFENDERS

The most commonly observed characteristic of the incest offender is extreme self-centeredness. The offender exhibits poor impulse control, sometimes acting out in violent, unpredictable, or immature behavior. He has low self-esteem and low ego strength. While he may dominate his family, he may be mild mannered and likable to those outside of the unit. He maintains his incest relationship with the child by various means including threats, bribes, manipulation, and intimidation. He has few social skills and often feels discomfort in relationships with adult females. The experiences of his life are carried with him into the marriage relationship and parenting role. It is as though he is a time bomb. The tensions he experiences are expressed in various ways, such as: suicidal gestures, substance abuse, exhibitionist behavior, voyeuristic offenses, and abusing children. The incest very often has been of long-term duration. It may have been only one year, but six or seven years is not unusual.

It is difficult to evaluate what motivates an offender to seek therapy for behavior change. Fear of society's sanctions is undoubtedly part of that motivation. Some clients, however, come to therapy without involvement in the criminal justice system — about 10 percent — and they frequently continue after the family system is no longer an issue, demonstrating a sincere desire to change behavior.

Not all offenders can be treated in a counseling agency environment by the therapist. The incest offender who is not accepted as a client at the Center is : (a) the diagnosed psychopath who is an exploitative offender where his sexual needs preempt all else, that is he simply does not care; (b) the pedophile, or the man who is fixated on a young sexual partner and cannot, and does not, want to achieve sexual gratification with an adult; (c) the aggressive pedophile, the person who obtains gratification by cruel and vicious assaults, usually on boys; and, (d) the offender who totally denies any possibility of incestuous involvement. These individuals are referred to other sources, e.g., psychiatrists, the criminal justice system, etc.

The decision as to whether a client is appropriate for therapy at CASA is determined in the initial screening sessions. This can take from one to as many as six sessions depending on the situation. Those offenders accepted at CASA are required to (a) make a commitment to engage in therapy, (b) define specific goals to be achieved, and (c) recognize and accept responsibility for the sexual assault. During these sessions there is also the necessity to ascertain the needs of the other family members and contact support systems required, e.g., criminal justice, child protective services, and welfare.

OFFENDER TREATMENT AT CASA

When the offender arrives at the intake session, the level of admission and denial of the incest varies from client to client. Generally there is a strong denial of reality. Few violators admit guilt initially. Rather, there are alibis. For example: "If I did do it, I don't remember"; "I must have blacked out"; or, "I was stoned." The therapist should be candid and direct. The therapist must be honest with the data available, sharing with the offender the available information, e.g., "Your daughter says...," "Your wife says..." The reports may be read to describe exactly what is charged.

Children rarely lie about incest. In a total treatment population of more than 400 families at CASA, only two fathers were falsely accused. These men gave very different responses to the charges and resultant crisis than did the offenders. The falsely accused men expressed grave concern for the psychological health of the child and a willingness to do whatever was necessary to help. They were "other" centered, concerned with the child, rather than with themselves. The guilty offender, on the other hand, usually displays many of the following characteristics: tenseness, wariness, fearfulness, apprehension, and tearfulness. Often he will make suicidal gestures, be involved in substance abuse, and threaten anyone who confronts him.

The person who agrees to therapy comes with the presenting problem of sexual assault, but there are many other problems normally needing to be addressed. Incest is identified as a symptom of a dysfunctional family, a family in pain and conflict. The incest offender is not crazy, there are reasons for his behavior. However, these reasons are not allowed to be excuses. The therapist must facilitate awareness for the client, confront him with the reality of his situation, and offer alternative behaviors. The incest offender is despite his denial, more keenly aware of his "abnormal" behavior than nonoffenders. He possesses low self-esteem and is constantly reinforcing this self-image with negative messages. Frequently this self-contempt is projected outward onto others.

The incest offender must recognize his capacity for change. He must experience making choices and controlling impulses. He needs to build and use a support system of family, therapist, friends, co-workers, and group members. The critical element is support, not dependence. Ultimately the client must come to believe in himself through enhancement of his self-concept. Self-esteem and self-control are nourished by practice, time, and understanding.

Almost every client lives with questions such as the following. "Why did I do it?" "Will I do it again?" "Can I stop?" "Am I a monster?" "Have I injured my child, perhaps permanently?" Each must come to responsible resolution of these issues. With awareness, education, safeguards, goals, and practice, positive mental health can be developed. The client needs to recognize he was meeting his own need through the child without consideration of consequences for the child or others involved.

Immediate Treatment Concerns

The immediate therapeutic need is to begin building safeguards against the incest behavior reoccuring. An example of such a technique would be always carrying 25¢ in his pocket to call the therapist or another significant person when he feels like offending. The client should learn to substitute other behaviors and to appropriately channel the drive for stimulation he experiences via sublimated activities such as hang gliding, parachute "free fall," or motorcycles. This change does not usually occur dramatically, but is shaped with constant reinforcement.

The offender needs to learn to problem-solve one step at a time. He faces a multiplicity of possible repercussions, including losing his job, his family, his reputation and going to jail. If, during this crisis time, an intact family presents too many stresses, the offender should be urged to absent himself from the home. The removal of the offender, rather than the child from the home, focuses responsibility for the activity to the parent. Therefore, the child is less isolated, and disruption in daily routines is minimized. Additionally, the problems frequently associated with foster care such as placement, expense, and monitoring are avoided. The child should be removed only as a last resort.

Briefly, after the initial individual sessions, the offender joins a weekly offenders' support group. Mothers, children, and other family members are seen individually and will often join one of the groups as well. Work with offenders involves a team concept and clinical staffing of cases with other involved professionals. If there is a need for specific expertise, such as in substance abuse, gender identity confusion, or severe dysfunctioning, consultation with others should be made.

Ongoing Treatment Issues

Several issues are raised in the treatment of offenders. One is working with the criminal justice system. Honest cooperation is an absolute necessity. All states have some type of mandatory reporting laws. It is a Class Two misdemeanor in Arizona if a professional fails to report to Child Protective Services, or police, knowledge of physical or sexual abuse; punishable by $1000 fine and/or six months in jail. The therapist should always report. To do otherwise is both legally and ethically questionable. A therapist can still be effective and interact with the criminal justice system if honest with the clients.

The second issue is transference and countertransference. The understanding, directive role of the incest therapist is a logical environment for transference to occur. The therapist should be alert for this, and if it happens, be honest about it with the client. The therapist may hear, "You're the only person who understands me...," "You have beautiful eyes...," "Can I take you to dinner...?" This is an opportunity to model appropriate nonsexual relationships with adult females (assuming the therapist is female) and talk about how the client can do this with other females. Countertransference, or being attracted to the client, is also a hazard with incest therapy. Many incest clients are facing extreme life crises and it is natural for the therapist to be impacted by the client's needs. The therapist cannot do it for them and must not become overinvolved. Objectivity is critical.

A counselor working with incest offenders must be a balanced blend of therapist and police officer. The therapist must also be concerned for the optimal mental health of the client and use whatever interventions deemed appropriate to effect positive mental health. The expression of positive regard for the client as a person, sensitivity to his moods, his pain, and his needs are certainly included in these techniques. However, concurrent with this, the therapist represents society's values, mores, and laws. Thus, the therapist must identify and clarify the sanctions that can be imposed for incestuous behavior. There is no client-counselor confidentiality in Arizona, other than that between lawyer and client. The therapist or records can, and frequently are, supoenaed into court. This information should be shared with the client at the onset of treatment if applicable to individual state regualtions.

DISCUSSION

Offender therapy can be likened to building a house. The foundation is set in initial individual sessions. The walls are built in the Offenders' Group in preparation for sessions with other family members. The roof of the house is family therapy with father, mother, and children. To keep the house from tumbling down in the future, all parts must be sturdy and secure. It is important to remember that even if the primary family is fragmented, the offender will alsmost certainly go on to become a member of another family unit. If he is involved in therapy, this will be true. If he goes to jail, this will be true. If he just goes unidentified, this will be true.

With these ideas in mind, the CASA staff extend a strong effort to implement an integrated treatment approach to help the incest offender, and family.

MOTHERS IN INCESTUOUS FAMILIES

Margot B. Zuelzer
Richard E. Reposa

ABSTRACT: Based on the premise that mothers in father-daughter incest families are pivotal in the incestuous bond, this article considers the incestuous mother's personality dynamics and role within the context of parent-child nuclear and extended family interaction. Such fundamental issues as separation-individuation, identification, and fear of intimacy are addressed from a developmental perspective. Patterns of functioning of mothers who are both victims and colluders are highlighted, followed by treatment implications.

Incest as a social and psychological phenomenon has become an area of increasing social concern. Overall, clinical perspectives regarding individual and family dynamics have changed over the years (Guthiel and Avery, 1972). Work in the area of incest was initially based on a unidimensional, epidemiological, descriptive perspective, which perceived the child essentially as victim of a parental sexual deviate. This view expanded to a psychologically investigative one, which conceptualizes incest as a collusive act, where the adult proponents (i.e., the parents) are driven to repeat childhood experiences or conflicts interactionally with the child, who may be an active, even seductive, participant. The developmentally most recent, family process perspective, sees incest as an attempted, although admittedly dysfunctional, solution to con-

Margot Zuelzer, Ph.D., is Assistant Professor, Department of Psychiatry, University of Texas Health Science Center, 7703 Floyd Curl Drive, San Antonio, TX 78229. Richard Reposa, M.S.W., is Social Psychotherapist at the Community Guidance Center, 2135 Babcock Road, San Antonio, TX 78229. Reprint requests may be sent to Dr. Zuelzer at the above address.

International Journal of Family Therapy 5(2), Summer 1983
0148-8384/83/1400-0098$02.75©1983 Human Sciences Press

flicts and disequilibria in the family as a whole (Matchotka, 1967; Nagy and Spark, 1973). All members are relevant etiologically, even those generally perceived as peripheral because they do not overtly engage in incestuous contact. Although originally ignored as an innocent bystander and victim, the mother in such families is perceived more and more to be the pivot in the establishment of the father-daughter incestuous bond (Guthiel and Avery, 1972).

Accepting the premise that an individual's functioning can be fully understood only from an interactional viewpoint, a look at such important questions as: What is the role of the mother in father-daughter incest families? How did she end up as colluder and victim? And what are the implications for treatment of such women? highlights the importance of considering the mother's personality dynamics within the context of parent-child, nuclear, and extended family interactions. Thus, a complex model of multiple levels must include an understanding of the individual, family subsystems, the nuclear family, and the family of origin.

INCESTUOUS MOTHERS AND THE FAMILY OF ORIGIN: A DEVELOPMENTAL PERSPECTIVE

Within all family systems, fundamental issues of human development, such as differentiation and separation-individuation must be newly addressed from generation to generation. Unless members in each generation learn to individuate and meet their own needs for contact and belonging in appropriate and affectionate relationships with other adults, a familial relationship system marked by fusion and undifferentiation results. Bowen (1971–1972) defines this multigenerational process as follows:

> The basic degree of differentiation of self is a rather fixed quality that is usually determined early in childhood by the degree of differentiation of the parents and by the prevailing emotional climate in the family of origin . . . one's own level of differentiation is replicated in marriage following which one's self is emotionally interlocked with parents in the past generation, the spouse in the present generation and children in the future gneration (p. 82).

Framo (1974) in his important work on the family of origin considers current marital and family difficulties to be extensions of relationship problems of the spouses in their original families.

He defines the family as an arena of individuation—where human beings learn about intimacy and boundaries. Lewis and Beavers (1978) describe healthy families as having the following characteristics: (1) They present a strong parental coalition with explicit boundaries between parents and children; (2) They enjoy open and clear communication among members; (3) They are able to share feelings openly, with predominance of positive affect; and (4) They are able to tolerate and respect growth and autonomy among family members.

In contrast, incestuous families present a clinical syndrome of parental dysfunction. For mothers in such families especially, closely linked identification with a harsh rejecting parent and with "bad" childhood figures predominate (Nakashima and Zakus, 1980). Most mothers, whether from "classic" (that is ingrown) incest families or from multiproblem families, are heavily dependent on their nuclear and extended family for contact and gratification of emotional needs. The seed of this is found in early development of the girl child.

Frances and Frances (1976) in *Incest Taboo and Family Structure,* see families in general as asymmetrical organisms, where different roles in child rearing result in different developmental pitfalls for boys and girls in the process of separation-individuation (and Oedipal development). Early symbiotic attachment between boys and girls and their mothers is the result of erotic gratification in the form of touch and nurturance through feeding, fondling and bathing, and by social interaction through signaling behavior and reciprocal responding. This generalizes to a more diffuse affectional bond within the individuation process between mother and child. The father, who has largely stayed outside of the symbiotic tie, now aids in the process of individuation from mother by becoming an object of identification for the boy, who disidentifies with the mother, but who retains her as a love object until resolution in the Oedipal period. The girl, who must also move outside the symbiotic relationship with the mother, takes the father as a love object, but never disidentifies with the mother, since she retains the feminine gender and role. Women, thus, never tend to achieve the degree of independence from their mothers or from later love objects that boys do. On the other hand, the father is the first stranger encountered outside the symbiosis, and it is from him that she learns to feel trustful of the outside world. The fact that females are more centered on relationships with their mothers and with love objects points to potentially devastating long-range relationship problems for the sexually abused girl.

Parents establish a model for identification through their behavior and values; the more powerful this model, the more likely daughters are to adopt the mother's conduct and values through the identification process. Slater (1961) outlined two different modes of identification in children. In "personal identification," the child adopts the values, attitudes, and personality attributes of a nurturant role model. This allows for the internalization of positive aspects of parents for a psychologically healthy development in males and females. In what he calls "positional identification," Slater (1961) states that as a defensive reaction to frustrations, lack of nurturance, and parental aggression, the child unconsciously wishes to destroy and replace the model as a matter of survival. Thus parental behavior that is interpreted as chronically rejecting or persecutory, forces the child, who is unable to change or give up the loved-hated object, to internalize these aspects as a psychological representation which eventually becomes part of the personality structure of the developing individual. During the course of development, other significant figures are assimilated into the inner (bad) object introjects. It follows, that when the child is an adult, the actions of others are perceived and interpreted largely in terms of internal needs and distorted expectations, while intimates, such as spouses and children, are, through projective identification, given similar faces and made to fulfill similar roles as the early parental figures who are so threatening and punitive, and therefore could not be given up (Fairburn, 1954).

Justice and Justice (1976) consider continuing symbiotic attachment of incestuous mothers to their families of origin, and through them to their spouses, a major problem. Functioning more often than not at a pregenital level, these women have in common a pervasive and childish need for nurturance and warmth. Never able to have given up the pathetic hope to obtain the mothering and protection they missed as small children, they will go to any length to satisfy their needs for affection, attention, and support, even if at the cost of their own children (Meiselman, 1978). Typically from an unstable family background, marked by emotional deprivation, and physical and/or psychological desertions by their own mothers, they suffer from strong anxiety and fear of family disintegration. Finkelhor (1980) refers to a pervasive kind of family emotional climate across generations, dominated by the fear of abandonment, which results either in withdrawal or in a continuing quest for closeness and fusion, superseding already weak generational and role boundaries.

Paradoxically, the fear of abandonment generates an intolerance for appropriate and rewarding intimacy. Feldman (1980) in his work on marital conflicts, describes an intimacy-conflict cycle, where unconscious anxiety in relation to interpersonal intimacy is seen as a major stimulus of interpersonal conflict behavior in marriages. When during the child's early years "the degree of actual and anticipated intimacy (of whatever kind, abandonment, punishment, exploitation) exceeds the upper limit of acceptable deviation, unconscious anxiety is stimulated that has to do with fears related to intimate contact" (p. 22), fear of abandonment, as one type of intimacy anxiety, at the preoedipal level generates feelings of being overwhelmed and helpless because of fear of loss of the love object. Thus, excessive or traumatic separations between mother and her small child are apt to create an unconscious link between separation and loss.

Adult experiences of intimacy may reawaken similar (unconscious) fears of loss, leaving the adult to defend either through withdrawal or through generating interpersonal conflict. The mother who was physically or psychologically abandoned by her own mother during her early years may withdraw from her own children or spouse and/or be combative in order to master this anxiety. Fear of abandonment during the Oedipal period tends to be complicated by the notion of rivalry between mother and daughter. To the extent that the daughter is successful in "winning" her father, the love and support of her mother is lost. In pathological development, generated by early incestuous relationships, this anxiety may persist unconsciously, and may surface whenever similar impulses are aroused during adult life. A counterphobic stance might make such a woman choose a similar sexual partner or mate over and over, no matter how dysfunctional, as long as he resembles her own incestuous father. Fear of persecutory attack and annihilation is caused by overwhelming frustration in response to a punitive, cold and rejecting early environment, which may stimulate the projection of intense, aggressive, destructive impulses onto the parent. Such fears if unresolved, will determine the structure of adult intimate relationships involving psychotic or borderline personality disorder mothers in incestuous families. Fear of exposure, due to a marked sense of inferiority and shame, may affect mothers as well as other members of incestuous families (since they generally experience themselves as weak and inadequate) thus leaving them to avoid or terminate close and intimate relationships. Fear of one's own destructive impulses, in the absence of resolution of depressive anxiety related to rage at a frustrating parent in early development, may result in a chronic depressive position. This may become a powerful potential stimulus for avoidance and defensive behavior regarding closeness between mothers, their spouses, and their children, in incestuous relationships.

MOTHER AS VICTIM AND COLLUDER: PATTERNS OF FUNCTIONING

In light of the strong bondage and relationship orientation of female children to their significant others (Frances and Frances, 1976) mothers and daughters across the generations are strongly affected by each other. Incestuous families are analogous to centripetal families (Beavers, 1977). Mothers are frequently present as dependent women who have adopted a masochistic stance and whose self-image is extremely low due to undifferentiated relationships with their own mothers, characterized by rejection and hostility. Maternal grandmother, in many cases, has been sexually abused herself during childhood and/or adolescence. Enraged with her own father who was experienced by her as either abusive or sexually exploitative, and with her own mother for not protecting her or not being emotionally accessible to her, thus having to turn to her father to compensate for lack of mothering, grandmother will vent her rage consciously or unconsciously on the daughter by being punitive, overcontrolling, rejecting, or by being physically or emotionally unavailable. Meiselman (1978) mentions in her book *Incest*, the possibility that incest is a "transmissible phenomenon," where the incestuous daughter may re-enact her mother's role and set her own daughter up for incest. Identification with the masochistic stance of the mother will not allow the daughter to actively work out expressed dissatisfactions regarding her marriage, which usually is poorly integrated and experienced as frustrating. As a result of early incest experiences within disturbed families, fear of intimacy may cause long-term problems with sexual identity and sexual responsiveness which frustrate and deprive the husband, and make such women "incest carriers" across generations (Meiselman, 1978 p.217), Sgroi et al (1982) found incestuous mothers both psychologically and physically absent as mothers and wives. Dependent mothers who would stay close to home would fail to set limits and protect their daughter by either ignoring their husband's open and flagrantly inappropriate behavioral interaction with the daughter (such as wrestling on the floor, sleeping in the same bed with the child, seeing the child naked on her father's lap, etc.) and/or leaving the room physically. Often alcoholism or chronic illness was part of the picture.

In our experience such mothers tend to exhibit lack of psychological investment in their children, either due to their own early emotional deprivation or lack of social skills. Their needs to be taken care of are so primary and profound, that they have to turn to their children for support in a demanding physical and emotional role reversal. Never having had a viable female model to learn negotiation and compromise, these mothers are unable to communicate effectively with husband and children, other than in a controlling, coercive, punitive, critical and nonsupportive way. Nor can they make effective contact with the outside world, since they more often than not have learned as children to avoid responsibility for their own thoughts, feelings, and actions by projecting blame either on their parents, siblings and/or the outside world. As adults, they tend to perpetuate this mode of functioning. Coming from a closed family system, they help recreate a similar one. Denial and repression of the realities of their family dysfunction and of their emotional pain is in the service of their own fragile self-esteem, and in the way they have typically learned to deal with unresolvable conflict in their early life. Authority is the bond between family members, and the myth that all is well "if you do what is right" pervades life. Thus the mother's collusion, which is in the service of maintaining the marriage and family bond by sanction is violated-through the daughter's initial attempts to let mother know about the incest, mother is prone to ignore, deny or be punitive. "Shut up—you liar—you know he (father) wouldn't do such a thing," was the reaction of the mother of a five year old. If the daughter tells someone else, mother is prone to scapegoat the child: "Look what you have done to our family. Your father is going to lose his job and will go to jail. Our family will be broken up. I guess you wanted that," one mother said to her 11-year-old daughter, who had reported the incest to the school counselor.

A mother that is part of a multiproblem family analoguous to Beavers' (1977) centrifugal model will most likely be involved in chaotic and shifting patterns of dominance between marriage partners and transient coalitions between herself and her children, as she experienced her family of origin. Mother, father, and children will use the family as a context for the manipulative, exploitative techniques. Individual family members are scapegoated incessantly, while projection, blaming, and attacking shifts continually between family members. Incestuous behavior may be cross-generational with total lack of boundaries, involving father, grandfather, and all the children. Explosiveness, argumentativeness, and hostility between family members mask depressive and anxiety states which are rarely confronted. As these rise, the inappropriate and undersocialized behavior of children and parent accelerates. Just like the dependent mother, these women are not available emotionally and physically to their children. They show lack of empathy and largely ignore emotional pain. Less housebound and more dominant than their dependent counterparts, they unconsciously may use illness or their absence from the family as escapes from responsibility. Alcohol dependence and drug usage or prostitution may be other means to camouflage depression. Such mothers will collude by ignoring blatantly inappropriate and provocative sexual behavior in themselves and their family. Denial pervades their functioning. They usually are punitive with their daughters and may feel strong competition, as the daughter develops sexually. Frustrating and conflict ridden relationships between generations prevail, and the children are prone to recreate such relationships in their own families as adults. Usually the eldest daughter is forced to take over her mother's role sexually and as family caretaker. During adolescence, such children may resort to running away, drug usage, alcohol, promiscuity and finally leave home, whereupon a younger sister may be pressed by the father, with collusion by the mother, to take over the caretaking role of the older sibling. Where mother had made herself totally absent, through desertion, illness, or death, the daughter will assume the total mothering of her siblings, as well as the role of sexual partner for the father, and continue the mode of family interaction. Should the father bring in another woman, the daughter will not only have difficulty giving up her preferential relationship with her father, but also her control as a mother over the siblings.

In most incestuous families, where mothers are unable to take adult marital and parenting responsibilities, incestuous relationships are tolerated by daughters, often since early childhood, and denied by the colluding mother for years, in a combined, unconscious effort to keep the family together.

Nagy (1973), in his work *Invisible Loyalties,* finds that the most fundamental loyalty commitment of family members pertains to the maintenance of the group. Such commitment goes beyond conscious behavioral manifestations. What seems to be shockingly destructive behavior on the part of one family member toward another—such as the role of the colluding mother toward her daughter—may not be consciously experienced as such by the participants, if the behavior conforms to a basic family loyalty—i.e., keeping the family together. The role of the daughter is clear. As Framo (1974) states:

> For the sake of approval by the parents and because abandonment has such disastrous consequences, the child will sacrifice whatever ego integrity is called for in order to survive. If the price for acceptance is to absorb unrealities, accept an irrational identity or role assignment...this price will have to be paid. To be alone or pushed out of the family either physically or psychologically is too unthinkable (p.207).

During adolescent struggles related to separation-individuation, these daughters may turn outside the family for help. Their guilt at breaking up the family is greater than their guilt and shame about the incest (Rosenfeld et al, 1977). Given what we have learned, the likelihood is great that these daughters as adult spouses and mothers will carry the burden of such strong and conflicted bondage into old age and pass it on to their daughters, unless the cycle can be broken.

Roland Summit (1982) has said it eloquently:

> Every child of incest deserves a mother who can understand her daughter's position without feeling betrayed or resentful. Every child deserves a mother who can make a clear choice for protection of her child without prejudice, even if it means severing an otherwise rewarding adult relationship. Every woman who discovers that her husband has taken her daugh-

ter as a sexual partner deserves help in sorting out her own reactions to such an assaultive discovery. And every mother who has been a partner to incestuous assault, no matter how passive or unwitting her role may have been, should be evaluated by professionals who are sensitive to the dynamics of child abuse before it is assumed that she is ready to assume protective responsibility for her children, with or without the assistance of the designated offender (p.147).

TREATMENT IMPLICATIONS

According to Ivan Nagy (1973) "In the treatment of (incestuous) families the mere demonstration of family dynamics or pathogenic forces is not enough. Open admission of the fact that incest is not the final goal in treatment, nor does it of necessity lead to changes." An evaluation of the wounds of exploitation and mutual victimization in the nuclear and family of origin, as well as a sensitive ongoing exploration of mutual caring, concerns, affection, and wishes for finding safer foundations for closeness between family members is indicated. Nagy's observations coincide with our treatment experience.

The nuclear family is usually subdivided into parent-child, husband-wife, subsystems, with a third subsystem consisting of parents and members of the family of origin. Invariably, symptoms in one subsystem may be reactions to conflicts pertaining to the other. For instance, disturbed parent-child or husband-wife interaction is evoked by the parent's (or mate's) associating a problem or a feeling which he/she had in childhood toward his or her own parents over similar issues. Unfortunately, Meiselman (1978) found in 50 years of research that backgrounds of mothers in father-daughter incest cases were seldom explored by therapists, since mothers were not usually the identified patients. Exploration of such family of origin conflicts and experiences becomes crucial in understanding the dynamics of interaction between all family members, but especially between the collusive parent and child. Desired changes in the family system must in the end involve realignment of the coalition between father-daughter to husband-wife, and the creation of a new, more appropriate father-daughter relationship, and more viable mother-daughter coalition through changes in role-definition in which the family members assume more appropriate role and generational boundaries. Such changes, in order to be effective and permanent, cannot be separated from internal experiences and changes in each family member.

While approaching the family as a system, empathetic awareness of each individual member's deep rooted needs and conflicts across generations related to dependency, separation/individuation, and intimacy becomes crucial in order to achieve more adaptive family functioning. Fraiberg (1980) in her pioneer work with infants and mothers has found that the recollection and reliving of feelings associated with early family of origin conflicts, centering on symbiotic attachments, fear of abandonment, and lack of nurturance enabled abusive mothers to respond more empathetically to their children. In our work, the family unit is used as the major forum for treatment as work is done within subsystems, such as the marital dyad, or parent-child dyad or triad. Where necessary, parallel group experiences for dependent mothers, or individual treatment for borderline or psychotic mothers or daughters (or other family members) may be indicated. Once the mothers within the subsystem are helped to confront previously inacessible and inadmissable memories of their childhood experiences and attitudes toward their parents and share these with spouse or child, their capacity for improved (that is, less projective interpersonal) functioning is dramatically heightened. reexamination of defensively avoided relational memories, such as exploitation of the colluding mother by her own father during childhood or scapegoating, putdown and physical and/or sexual mistreatment from either parent, may coincide with phasic intensification and shifts in positive or negative transference significance of the therapist.

The use of a male-female cotherapy team in the treatment will greatly facilitate this process, providing an interactional model of open and respectful communication through the treatment team, while allowing for the working through of intensive feelings with one therapist, in the "safe" presence of the other. Reparenting through the female therapist of mothers in such families who are in most cases still at the pregenital level, is a necessity and will result in a growth process which encompasses a renewed identification phenomenon, personal rather than positional, where mothers, daughters, and other family members work through hurt and anger. They then grow emotionally and therefore can assume more personal responsibility as mothers and more mature and

MARGOT B. ZUELZER, RICHARD E. REPOSA

functional relationships with their spouses. Ongoing facilitation of some corrective emotional experiences between husband and wife, as well as mother and child, as they try out their new roles and test new boundaries is needed in order to bring about a "realignment and rebalancing" (Nagy and Spark, 1973) of relationships within the family. Only long-term work with mothers and daughters along multilevel lines of intervention and support can in the final analysis help such women break the cycle of incest for themselves and their daughters to come.

REFERENCES

Beavers, W. R., *Psychotherapy and Growth. A Family Systems Perspective.* New York: Brunner/Mazel, Inc., 1977.

Boszormeny-Nagy, Ivan, and Spark, Geraldine. *Invisible Loyalties: Reciprocity in intergenerational Family therapy,* Hagerstown, Md.: Harper and Rowe, 1973.

Bowen, M. Toward the Differentiation of Self in One's Family of Origin. In F. D. Andres and J. P. Lorro (Eds.) *Georgetown Family Symposia: A Collection of Papers,* Volume 1 (1971–1972), Georgetown University Medical Center, Department of Psychiatry, 1974.

Fairburn, W. R. D. *An Object Relations Theory of the Personality,* New York: Basic Books, 1954.

Feldman, L. Mental Conflict and Marital Intimacy: An Integrative Psychodynamic-Behavioral-Systemic Model. In John G. Howells (Ed.) *Advances in Family Psychiatry II,* New York: Brunner/Mazel, 1980.

Finkelhor, D. Psychological, Cultural and Family Factors in Incest and Family Sexual Abuse. I. V. Cook and R. T. Bowles (Eds.) *Child Abuse: Commission and Ommission.* Toronto: Butterworth Co., 1980.

Fraiberg, Selma (Ed) *Clinical Studies in Infant Mental Health.* New York: Basic Books, 1980.

Framo, I. L. Family of Origin as a Therapeutic Resource for Adults in Marital and Family Therapy: You Can and Should Go Home Again. *Family Process,* 1974, *15,* 2.

Frances V. and Frances A. The Incest Taboo and Family Structure. *Family Process.* 1976, *15,* 2.

Gil, David. First steps in a Nationwide Study of Child Abuse.*Social Work Practice,* 1966, pp. 61–78.

Guthiel, T. G., And Avery, N. C. Multiple overt incest as family defense against loss. *Family Process,* 1977, *16,* (1) 105–116.

Justice, B. and Justice R. *The Abusing Family,* New York: Human Sciences Press, 1976.

Lewis, J. M., Beavers, W. R., et al. *No Single Thread: Psychological Health in Family Systems.* New York: Brunner/Mazel Inc., 1976.

Machotka, P. et al. Incest as a Family Affair. *Family Process,* 1967, 6, 98–116.

Meiselman, Karen C. *Incest: A Psychological Study of Causes and Effects with Treatment Recommendations.* Josse Basse, Inc., San Francisco, 1978.

Nakashima, I. Zakus, G. Incest: Review and Clinical Experience. In J. V. Cook and R. T. Bowles (Eds.) *Child Abuse: Commission and Omission.* Toronto: Butterworths Co., 1980.

Sgroi, Susan and Dana, Natalie. Individual and Group Treatment of Mothers of Incest Victims. In Susan Sgroi (Ed.) *Handbook of Clinical Intervention in Child Sexual Abuse,* Lexington Books, 1982.

Slater, P. E. Toward a dualistic theory of identification. *Merrill Palmer Quarterly* 1961, *7*, 113.
Summit, Ronald. Beyond Belief: The Reluctant Discovery of Incest. In Martha Kirkpatrick
(Ed.) *Women's Sexual Experience: Exploration of the Dark Continent.* New York:
Plenum Press, 1982, p.147.

FAMILY THERAPY WITH INCEST

Richard E. Reposa
Margot B. Zuelzer

ABSTRACT: Intervention to interrupt the cycle of incest poses unique considerations for the clinician. This paper presents a multilevel intervention model making use of the family system and subsystems within it to interrupt the incest cycle. The discussion provides a perspective for the clinician for intervention with such families including the use of dyads: Husband-wife, father-daughter, mother-daughter. It focuses on the central importance of strengthening the marital dyad while providing support for realignment of dysfunctional coalitions which allowed for the emergence of the incest cycle. Boundaries, collusion, the use of the therapy team, and implications for treatment are integral to the discussion.

The incest phenomenon has been the focus of study by sociologists, anthropologists, and more recently, clinicians. It has evoked a range of cognitive and emotional responses by those involved in efforts to understand its impact on human functioning from recognition and acknowledgement to retraction, avoidance, denial, and more recently, concerted efforts by clinicians to conceptualize an effective means of intervention not only for the victim and perpetrator, but also for those less directly affected by the incest experience, the members of the family in which the incest has occurred. This paper will delineate a multilevel mode of intervention which has its center a family system frame for both

Richard Reposa, M.S.W. is a Social Psychotherapist at the Community guidance Center, 2135 Babcock Road, San Antonio, TX 78229. Margot B. Zuelzer, Ph.D., is Assistant Professor, Department of Psychiatry, University of Texas Health Science Center, 7703 Floyd Curl Drive, San Antonio, TX 78229. Reprint requests may be sent to Mr. Reposa at the above address.

International Journal of Family Therapy 5(2), Summer 1983
0148-8384/83/1400-0111$02.75©1983 Human Sciences Press

112

INTERNATIONAL JOURNAL OF FAMILY THERAPY

understanding and intervening in the unique dynamics of the incest family.

The early struggles of Freud to understand the origin and presence of an incest taboo and to confront its breakdown continue to be crucial as a first step in the attempts by clinicians to intervene with the incest family. In his work, *The Etiology of Hysteria,* Freud (1896) concludes: "I therefore put forward the thesis that at the bottom of every case of hysteria there are one or more occurrences of premature sexual experiences, occurrences which belong to the earliest years of childhood" (p.203). This position was later partially rejected by Freud, a modification necessary to relieve the anxiety of his fellow therapists. The struggles of Freud serve as a reminder to clinicians that intervention with the incest family begins with acknowledgment by the therapist that such events are a reality, and that intervention of a multilevel nature is indicated. It is of crucial importance both for the victim and her family that acknowledgment be clear and consistent by the therapist throughout the course of treatment.

FAMILY SYSTEMS

As essential as acknowledgment of the presence of incest on the part of both the clinician and his patients is the assumption that such interactions take place within a context which is the family system. Incest then becomes symptomatic of family system dysfunction, and while intervention for the remediation of such dysfunction will occur on many levels, it is the family system which must be carefully used as a barometer of both growth and regression.

Beavers (1977) in *Psychotherapy and Growth,* provides a comprehensive exploration of the variables which determine levels of family system functioning. He delineates ranges of family functioning extending from the healthy family to the midrange family and finally to the severely dysfunctional family. The essential qualities of living systems, including establishment of boundaries, a concept of time and space, a hierachy of values, and finally a capacity for adaptation, serve as indicators for the clinician of the level of family functioning and allow for the establishment of realistic and reachable therapeutic goals.

The healthy family system is characterized by such qualities as: a high degree of individual responsibility for feelings, thoughts, and actions; clear and consistent boundaries and overall family structure; a varied, less stereotypical family style; a predominantly positive mood; a climate of openness and clear expression of all feelings; a capable parental coaliton with a commensurate balance of power; and finally, the encouragement of autonomy. It is this set of qualities which the therapist seeks to promote in the course of intervention with families.

The midrange family system, which accounts for the majority of families which the clinician encounters, is characterized by appropriately open and closed boundaries between roles and generations; and an appropriate degree of cohesiveness, though these families may experience some difficulty with achieving a balance of cohesiveness and distance. The midrange family also promotes a healthy ongoing power struggle among its individual members for selfhood, and finally allows for a range of feeling tones, though the ability to incorporate such tones may at times appear somewhat stylized and stiff.

Finally, the severely disturbed family is characterized by an inability to assume responsibility for thoughts and actions, is inflexible, shows the absence of an adult parental coalition, approaches life stresses both within and outside the family in a helpless fashion characterized by indecisiveness. The degree of mutual dependency is high, while the ability of family members, and specifically adults, to empathize with other family members, is significantly impaired.

THE INCEST FAMILY

The importance of viewing a range of family functioning becomes central as the clinician attempts first to understand and then to intervene in the incest family system. In a study comparing abusive and nonabusive families Serrano, Zuelzer, Howe and Reposa (1979) compared 70 abusing and nonabusing families and tested Gil's hypothesis that "there are mainly differences in degree between abusing and nonabusing families" (p. 75). More specifically the same study compared the degree of involvement in abusing and nonabusing families and found a higher degree of overinvolvement between fathers and daughters in families where incest was present and a commensurate degree of underinvolvement between mothers and daughters in sexually abusing families than in control group families. What is crucial for the clinician intervening in incest families is the capacity to assess the degree of dysfunction in critical areas of family functioning, while also assessing the same in the individual family members in order that realistic goals can be set.

Among a number of dimensions of family functioning which appear critical for the clinician to assess, the following seem primary: (1) the capacity of the family for separation-individuation; (2) the capacity of the family to assert role and generational boundaries; (3) the nature of coalitions within the family system; and (4) the distribution of power and control in the family. If the notion of degree of pathology and function is accepted, then it becomes critical to view each of the above dimensions within that context. Beavers (1977) has carefully examined the separation patterns of families generally, and has described two patterns, both of which are relevant to an understanding of the incest family. According to Beavers, "Both styles of families, the centripetal group which binds children to the home and the centrifugal group which expels children in premature separation from family, have significant difficulty in handling object loss" (p. 89). Incest families experience separation as traumatic, perhaps as a re-enactment of earlier pain with separation on the part of parents, and so profoundly fear the possibility of separation not only of adults from children, but from each other as separate independent individuals who also happen to be part of the family. The fear of separation then allows the centripetal family to develop a series of coping mechanisms which are in the service of keeping the members of the family enmeshed and assist with allaying the fear of ultimate separation. Such families fight against all efforts at differentness, are unable to allow for appropriate development of functional subsystems within the family system, and manifest a pseudomutuality which again is in the service of precluding separation-individuation. Beavers asserts: "Centripetal families have a great fear that the pain in their families will be exposed to the broader community, and when such a family seeks treatment, it is usually by having one individual who defines himself as at fault and attempts to change" (p. 92). In incest families, it is often the victim who attempts to reach outside, and the dimension of blame and guilt which the victim feels becomes a critical therapeutic issue which must be attended to by the clinician, and one which other family members may often reinforce in the service of avoiding both responsibility and the need to deal with the issue of separation-individuation. Selby (1980) speaks of the difficulty with separation of incest families in stating, "A picture emerges of a family of unhappy people in which family members are unable to establish socially appropriate, separate, and satisfying relationships. This climate provides the milieu for the development of father/daughter incest... it would seem that once it has begun, the family tends to adopt protective measures" (p. 5).

Case Illustration

Sally, age 12, and her family were referred following allegations of incest between her and her stepfather. Mr. S. acknowledged the incest, while Mrs. S. asserted that "only S.'s father needed treatment." Efforts to involve the entire family were difficult, despite the fact that S.'s 16 year old brother had dropped out of school, was not working, and was "just hanging around the home." As the issue of the sexual abuse came to the fore, Mrs. S. retreated from the treatment, and threatened S. with "severe ramifications" if the sexual abuse was talked about further either in therapy or in the school.

The family has continued to deal with the issue of separation by becoming more and more closed, and currently individual intervention with Mr. S. is the only means available to reopen the family system to further intervention. The need to close the family and protect efforts at further separation both by Sally and other family members has only stiffened the dysfunctional boundaries between the family and the outside world.

Currently, efforts are being devoted to increasing the competence of one family member to open the family to further involvement by the therapists.

Beavers (1977) describes a second pattern of separation found in the centrifugal family. "Centrifugal families in contrast have flamboyant and repeated interpersonal crises spilling out into the larger community. These dramatic episodes serve to maintain the equilibrium in the centrifugal family system" (p. 92).

Case Illustration

A., age 15, her 13-year-old sister, and 11-year-old brother, were living with their father and stepmother and were referred by the child protection agency following multiple runaways involving all three children, one of which resulted in the children's attempting to move in with a neighborhood family. Repeated calls to the caseworker by neighbors following fights among family members, specifically between father and stepmother during bouts with drinking, had singled the family out as the "crazy family" in the community. A long-term incestuous involvement between father and all three children soon became apparent. It was also soon apparent that stepmother had not really "joined" with the family, did not see herself as part of the family, and made only sporadic attempts to involve herself in the family. She remained separate from the rest of the family much of the time.

A consistent runaway pattern by all three children and their attempts to reach out both to the caseworker and community at large constituted explosive separations from the family. Each episode was followed by efforts by the father particularly to retrieve the deviant family members and bring them back into the family system. Ultimately, the focus of family therapy was on assisting family members with developing more functional means of separation, which included in the case of the oldest daughter, finding employment outside the home which necessitated living in her place of employment, and in the case of the youngest child, a forced separation from the family with psychiatric hospitalization to interrupt both the cycle of abuse and also to diminish the possibility of further explosive separations.

A second critical dimension of dysfunction in the incest family is the inability of family members, and particularly adults, to assert clear and consistent role and generational boundaries. The lack of boundaries in such families may emerge in response to stress, or in more severely disabled families may be of a transgenerational nature. The lack of generational boundary assertion contributes significantly to the cycle of abuse, and hence assumes a position of central importance in the hierarchy of therapeutic goals with incest families. As has been stated previously, the incest families often build rigid and impermeable boundaries between themselves and the outside world, while internally allowing in many instances a fluidity which is dysfunctional and nonprotective. It is this inability to assert functional boundaries that contributes further to the isolation already felt by incest families vis-a-vis the world around them.

Two dimensions of boundary assertion become critical in the treatment of the incest family: the first concerns the ability of the family to assert boundaries with the outside world, and the second the capacity of the family system to establish and maintain its own internal sense of functional boundaries.

Case Illustration

Eleven-year-old J., her parents, her ten-year-old brother, nine-year-old brother, seven-year-old sister, and two-year-old sister were referred with presenting problems of sexual exploitation of J. by her father extending over a period of two years. During the evaluation session, J's younger brothers began sharing with the therapy team interactions involving sexual contact between J. and her father which both had observed by peering through a window. J. was extremely anxious and appeared disordered in her thinking; Mr. B. was apprehensive and admitted that the sexual abuse had occurred, and Mrs. B. expressed fear that the family might fall apart. Early in treatment, Mrs. B. expressed the wish to "be a baby," described retreats into her "own little world," and described her daughter as very attentive to the needs and feelings of her father. In addition, Mrs. B. described a distant relationship between herself and her husband, the result of a "fear of becoming pregnant," and a nonexistent relationship between herself and her daughter, of which she asked, "What do I know about how to be a mother? My mother was always gone."

The lack of clearly defined internal boundaries within the family allowed for the inappropriate observation of activity between J. and her father. In addition, the inability to screen content by J.'s brothers resulted from extreme anxiety which all were feeling in response both to the possibility of family breakdown, as well as having had access to information which more clearly defined boundaries would have protected them from, namely, observation of interactions between J. and her father. In addition, Mrs. B.'s withdrawal into her own world afforded additional vulnerability not only for J., but for her father as well. Mrs. B.'s fear of pregnancy and her inability to establish boundaries competently both within the marital relationship, as well as in the mother-daughter relationship, added to a cumulative systemwide inability to clearly assert and maintain role and generational boundaries for the safety and well-being of all family members.

The healthy family system has a strong, clearly defined, and mutually acknowledged marital coalition, which allows for the assertion of protective and consistent boundaries between generations. In incestuous families the needs of the adult partners for nurturance, contact, and worth are so primary that the establishment of an adult marital coalition which presumes the mutual meeting of adult-to-adult needs is not possible.

The absence of a strong marital coalition often decreases the likelihood of an effective parental coalition; the one moves in tandem with the other. In healthy families, a strong marital coalition supports the stresses implicit in parenting, and in severely disabled families, the absence of a strong marital coalition further cripples the efforts at effective parenting. It is the strong marital coalition which is the cornerstone of all other attempts at providing growth producing structure within the family system. Within the context of strong marital and parental coalitions, the struggles for selfhood and an emerging sense of separateness become possible for all family members, but particularly for children.

Hence, a central goal of the family therapy process with the incest family is the establishment of a growing and strong adult coalition. The adult coalition generates energy for therapeutic changes within the incest family including: the assertion of boundaries, the clarification of roles, the maintenance of appropriate privacy and protection between generations, and the careful monitoring of emotional and cognitive information within the family system.

In healthy families, the nature of parent-child coalitions changes with the developmental needs of the child, and does not do so to the exclusion of the marital coalition. The nature of the father-daughter relationship changes in response to the needs of the daughter, as does the nature of the mother-daughter coalition. In incest families, the overinvolvement of father with daughter leaves the family, and specifically victim and her father, vulnerable to the possibility of incest.

A third series of coalitions within the family system involves the sibship. In healthy families, the sibship provides multiple supports for privacy, and the appropriate acquisition and use of power, both with each other and in relationships with adults, specifically parents. The sibship provides a secondary level of support for growth and separateness. In incest families, the sibship often assumes a primary role for the provision of support for growth, protection, and nurturance. Often sibs assume primary responsibility for provision of mothering, with the hope that by providing such to one's sibs, somehow one receives mothering for oneself.

RICHARD E. REPOSA, MARGOT B. ZUELZER

Case Illustration

N. and her five sibs ranging in age from 19 to eight were referred for family treatment when all but N.'s older sister were placed with a maternal aunt on a permanent basis following the incarceration of their father and the death of their mother.

N. commented during a family therapy session: "I was the mother to these kids for the last six months at least." When asked what that meant, she replied, "That meant I took care of Daddy for these kids; I was the one who went to him to ask for things for them. I took care of Daddy in a lot of ways." When asked to explain further, N. commented, "I took care of Daddy sexually for these kids, and he promised me that if I would be with him and satisfy him, then he would not lay a hand on the other children. I found out later that he had already laid a hand on the other children before he had made the promise to me."

Clearly demonstrated in the above case material is the role which the sibship assumes in incestuous families. A most difficult task for N. following her placement in the home of her extended family, after "blowing the whistle" on her father, involved her struggle to give up the role of mother with her sibs, and attempt to resume the tasks of teenage separation-individuation for herself.

The case material also reflects the importance of overt and covert coalitions within incest families. N.'s rage over having been duped by her father clearly demonstrates a covert agreement implicit in the coalition between N. and her father as sex partners. The incest relationship emerges from a family style often unconscious of negotiating covert coalitions within the family, which fosters and maintains the inappropriate involvement between father and daughter. The "giving over" dynamic plays a crucial role in the repeat phenomenon so often seen in the incest family and perpetuates the cycle of abuse. Such "giving over" assists mother with discharging unresolved rage which she continues to feel toward her own father as a victim.

A final dimension of functioning in the incest family system involves the distribution of power and control within the family. It is critical to view power in the context of emotional competence. R.W. White (1966) has defined competence in a manner which seems particularly relevant to the incest family when he says, "With competence, an individual negotiates from a position of shared overt power, relying neither on intimidation nor helplessness for success" (p. 330). The issue of covert vs. overt power, its relationship to helplessness, and a lack of felt ability on the part of all family members, but particularly the victim, perpetrator, and colluder, to assume appropriate and effective power within the family are critical in intervention with the family. If power can be reframed as energy for competence, the goal of family therapy with the incest family then becomes one of increasing appropriate and mutually acknowledged competence in the context of careful consideration of developmental needs both for the family unit and the individual member as well.

Case Illustration

Mr. R. was being seen on an individual basis in conjunction with conjoint marital and family therapy. During a session in which Mr. R. expressed continuing confusion over how it was that he had done what he had done to his daughter, he began reflecting that shortly before the incest had begun, a number of stresses were present in the family. He recalled feeling more and more "cut off" from his wife, and he had been laid off from his job. Mr. R. expressed anger over the fact that his wife rebuffed his need for sexual contact with the message, "Perhaps you have a sex problem." He then shared the feeling that "at least I could feel powerful with my daughter, and besides that she would never reject me."

The incest relationship provided an opportunity for safety from rejection, as well as an opportunity to feel competent in the midst of multiple failures. The covert power which Mr. R. made use of in his relationship with his daughter was also in the service of dealing with the anger he felt toward his wife whom he saw as shutting him off sexually, and to that extent the control he had was mobilized out of anger and fear.

TREATMENT IMPLICATIONS

In the concluding section of this paper, clarification and delineation of specific modes of intervention within the treatment of an incest family will be discussed.

The diagnostic phase involves at least one session in which all family members are present to assess the overall family functioning and climate in which the incest emerged. It is critical during the initial session to encourage the family to provide their version of the events which brought the family to treatment. It is also important simply to observe interactions between family members, carefully note quality and nature of coalitions, and assess the means which the family uses to cope with the stress of the diagnostic process. It is also critical, at this point in the treatment, for the therapy team to begin assessing the developmental level of the family system, as well as the individuals.

Case Illustration

During the initial session, the younger brothers of J., an 11-year-old incest victim, revealed to the therapists that they had "seen things between J. and her father through the window." Efforts to assert boundaries on the content offered in the session were difficult. Anxiety manifested itself in the family and was apparent in individuals. J. sat anxiously beside her mother, made infrequent eye contact with the therapists, and appeared disorganized in her thinking. Mr. B. appeared extremely anxious, acknowledged the abuse, and was clearly overwhelmed by the presence of both the therapists and the caseworker, whom he viewed as authorities potentially effecting the integrity of his family. When asked how she would like things to be, Mrs. B. replied to the female therapist, "I want to be a baby."

The therapeutic process differs with the needs and coping styles of each family. In the above mentioned family, a treatment contract was formulated which involved establishing as quickly as possible areas of common concern, identifying differing coping mechanisms used by the family and by individuals, and redirectly the energy invested by Jane and her father in the incest relationship to a different sphere of interaction. Efforts were made to support Jane's academic competence. Mr. B.'s acknowledgment that "Jane is like me in that way" was used by the therapists to support intellectual interaction between Jane and her father. In addition, specific work was done to attempt to bridge Jane's worry and concern for members of her family and specifically her siblings to first explore the role reversal and then exlore the extent to which Jane and her mother could be involved differently with each other.

The goal of the diagnostic and early treatment phase was two-fold: first, to reframe the incest as a family problem to the extent that it somehow seemed to reveal the family's response to stress; second, to distinguish clearly between a family response to stress and ultimate responsibility for the incest as solely an adult issue. Meiselman (1978) speaks to the danger of the family therapy approach in this regard when she states, "A second, more subtle problem can occur with the family therapy approach to incest cases—the child's guilt can actually be increased by the therapeutic process. Commonly, a family therapist takes the spoken or unspoken stance that all family members are equally responsible for the family's difficulties and thus all of them are responsible for work toward a healthy family equilibrium. . . . If the family therapy approach is used, the therapist should emphasize repeatedly to the children that nothing they may have done justified the parent's behavior." (pp. 342, 343).

This potential pitfall can be avoided if efforts are made by the therapist to assist both partners with assuming responsibility for their role in the incest incident. Just as energy must be devoted to avoid isolating the child with guilt, so energy must be invested by the therapist to insure that the perpetrator not be left to bear all responsibility for the emergence of the incestuous relationship.

Case Illustration

Mr. and Mrs. B. were seen as a couple during the diagnostic phase. Mrs. B. expressed concern, dismay, and a feeling of being overwhelmed by the family crisis. Mrs. B. shared confusion over, "What does a daughter know about how to be a wife?" Mrs. B. described a distant relationship with her own mother, who was involved outside in the home caring for a handicapped sibling who spent much time in the hospital. Mrs. B. assumed many of the adult responsibilities of the home, doing washing and cooking, and caring for her younger brothers and sister, as her mother was unavailable to do so. Mrs. B. commented, "Mothers were supposed to just cook and do the washing and that's all." Mr. B. suffered analogous rejections. Deprived of his father through death very early, he was put in the role of breadwinner for his mother and siblings, but maintained strongly dependent and approval seeking ties to his mother. Beneath his narcissistic stance, he felt rejected, paranoid, and chronically anxious. Strong needs for contact were disguised in a pseudocompetent stance. Mrs. B. described a stern relationship with her father, indicating intense fear of him when drinking. She indicated that she had not been able to date until she met her husband and later became pregnant. The couple married when she was 16. In this context, Mrs. B. also mentioned her current fear of again becoming pregnant and the desire to have no more children.

The couple interview and subsequent couple sessions focused on the emotional reparenting of both partners. The wish to be a baby shared by Mrs. B. was used frequently to support Mrs. B.'s own felt unmet dependency needs. In addition, Mr. B. was supported to slowly relinquish an initial narcissistic stance. The team used his self-acknowledged intellectual capacities to redirect the focus of his relationship with Jane. Critical was the modeling provided Mrs. B. by the female therapist, whom Mrs. B. experienced as a different kind of mother. This allowed her to begin building a mother-daughter coalition. Gradually, Mrs. B. was able to see herself as a "different kind of mother" to Jane than her mother had been to her.

Concurrently, the couple sessions were used to explore with the couple the nature of the marital relationship. The focus was on Mrs. B.'s premature taking on of responsibility as a result of marrying young and having a baby soon thereafter. Parallels were drawn to commonalities which Mrs. B. had with her daughter: both had assumed heavy burdens of responsibility early in life, Mrs. B. first in the role reversal in her family of origin, then her early pregnancy, and Jane in terms of having assumed responsibility for coping with and attempting to understand an inappropriate relationship with her father.

A critical goal throughout the course of family treatment with incest, but particularly in the initial phases, is assisting both adults with increasing their capacity for empathy. The therapists attempt to increase the ability of both parents to walk in the shoes of another, in this case their daughter. It is the capacity for empathy which enables the adults to acknowledge responsibility for the incest, to make appropriate reparations, and move tòward the ultimate goal of a full apology for both actions and feelings generated by the incest experience. The family sessions focus on parent-child issues with primary emphasis on realigning the mother-daughter and father-daughter coalitions. Work is done with each dyad with the other parent observing. Each person is given specific tasks as homework, to focus on shifting the nature of the coalition with their child. Mrs. B. was initially supported to simply involve Jane in learning to cook. The coalition between Jane and her father was shifted by focusing on his involvement with Jane's learning accomplishments.

Case Illustration

Mrs. B. described J. as the one who would greet her father upon his return from work. Mr. B. expressed frustration over not being able to communicate as effectively with his wife as he could with J., and efforts were made by the female therapist to support Mrs. B.'s beginning efforts at seeing herself as "smart," "able to make decisions." Support was provided

Mr. B. by the male therapist who modeled respect for Mrs. B.'s developing competence, while also supporting efforts made by Mr. B. to see his wife differently and acknowledge her increased ability to be involved with him. Mrs. B. verbalized sensitivity to the loss which her daughter must be feeling at this point. Mr. B. acknowledged the loss of the "old relationship" while developing a different relationship between himself and his wife. Mrs. B. also described feeling the need to retreat to her "own little world," feeling overwhelmed, wanting to "just block everything out."

Implicit in the material above is the dynamic of collusion by Mrs. B. Nurturing questions by the female therapist about the impact on both J. and Mr. B. at those times when Mrs. B. felt the need to be in her own "little world" allowed her to acknowledge her role as the colluder in the incest. It was during this phase of treatment that Mrs. B. was able to develop increased empathy and insight into the struggles of her daughter. It was also important for the therapist to understand the longterm effects of the incest experience on the sibship. Mr. B. expressed concern that his oldest son had recently been involved in inappropriate contact with female peers at school. Efforts were made to elicit strengths in Mr. B. which enabled him to become a "different kind of father" to his sons. A single family therapy session provided the impetus to shift the behavior which concerned Mr. B. on the part of his son. Careful monitoring and checking back with the couple during the split sessions served as the barometer of family change.

Periodic follow-up sessions were held with the family in an effort to monitor the long-term effects of the incest experiences and to support maintenance of gains made in therapy. Approximately 27 months after the initial evaluation and nine months following termination, a follow-up session was scheduled.

Case Illustration

Mrs. B. shared gains made in the marital rlationship as well as differences in J.'s relationship with her father. Mrs. B. commented that shortly before the session she had noted that J.'s behavior had changed; she seemed withdrawn, less involved with the family and commented, "I admit, a little fear did come over me, and I felt as though I wanted to go again into my own little world." Mrs. B. indicated that she struggled very hard to remain in the room, while J. indicated to both her parents that she was "being touched at school." Mrs. B. commented that she could allow herself to be frightened and be clear about needing to be with her daughter and her husband as the three of them dealt with the school regarding the incident, in contrast to the past when she "would have allowed her husband to handle the situation alone." Mrs. B. was sensitive to her daughter's fear of consequences and was able to assume a protective stance with J. She described returning home and reaching out to J. expressing a willingness to "do whatever is necessary so you won't have to be afraid."

The therapists supported Mrs. B.'s ability to make use of new coping mechanisms under stress, when confronting her own fears. Mr. B. was able to be supportive of his wife's new competence in her role as mother to Jane. He in turn expressed a different kind of concern and caring for his daughter: "The man does not know what kind of burden he's putting on his daughter. I want her to understand that I am heartily sorry for what I did. Only time will tell if she can come to forgive me. This is something she'll carry for the rest of her life, but how it affects her will be important."

Additional work remains particularly for Mrs. B. and J. in terms of unfinished business and some indications that without further monitoring, Mrs. B. might well set J. up for early pregnancy and a repeat of her own experience.

CONCLUSION

This discussion has attempted to highlight the dimensions of intervention with the incest family system. The orchestraton of such intervention implies a commitment on the part of the therapist to view incest in the context of the family, paying careful attention to the complexity of factors which allow for the emergence of the incest relationship and to the multilevel intervention necessary to assist the victim, perpetrator, colluder, and other members of the family with making the changes necessary to preclude revictimization. The mosaic of pain crossing generations deserves attention, only some of which will be attended to in the course of treatment. Perhaps it is the role of the family therapist carefully to weave interventions into the mosaic, with the help of the family, to increase the potential for more effective interpersonal contact, while respecting the need for careful attention to long-term healing of wounds suffered by the recovering family.

REFERENCES

Beavers, W. Robert. *Psychotherapy and Growth*: Brunner/Mazel: New York, 1977.

Burgess, Groth, Homstrom and Sgroi. *Sexual Assault of Children and Adolescents*. Lexington Books: Lexington, 1978.

Freud, Sigmund. The Etiology of Hysteria. In *The Standard Edition of the Complete Psychological Works of Sigmund Freud*. New York: Hogarth Press, 1962.

Meiselman, Karen C., *Incest*. Jossey-Bass: San Francisco, 1978.

Selby, J.W. et al. Families of Incest: A collection of Clinical Impressions. *The International Journal of Social Psychiatry*, Volume 26, I, 1980.

Serrano, A.C., Zuelzer, M.B., Howe, D.D., and Reposa, R.E., Ecology of Abusive and Nonabusive Families. *Journal of Child Psychiatry*, 1979, 75.

White, R.W. Motivation reconsidered: the concept of competence. *Psychological Review*, 66 (5).

The Role of Group Therapy in Incest Counseling

Carol Fowler
Susan R. Burns
Janet E. Roehl

ABSTRACT: The use of group therapy is an essential component in the treatment program for victims of incest, their families, and offenders at the Center Against Sexual Assault in Phoenix, Arizona. Four types of groups are conducted on a continuous basis: (a) adults who were victims as children, (b) families of victims, (c) offenders, and (d) child victims. Group therapy is the predominant treatment modality for the 400 incestuous families seen at CASA. Details of each of the four groups are given in this article.

Group counseling is an interpersonal process where a counselor and several clients examine themselves and their life situations in an attempt to modify behavior and attitudes. (Hansen, Warner & Smith, 1976). Group counseling may be preventive and/or remedial for a client. With incest as a presenting problem, this approach can be more therapeutic than individual counseling. One of the values of the group process is that it provides a situation where an individual can receive immediate feedback from others in the group. The group experience affords members an opportunity to discuss concerns and establish genuine

Carol Fowler, M.A., M.C., is Associate Director of the Center Against Sexual Assault at 1131 East Missouri, Phoenix, AZ 85014. Susan R. Burns is President, Board of Directors at the Center. Janet E. Roehl, Ph.D., is in the Division of Continuing Education, University of Wisconsin-Stout, Menomonie, WI 54751. Reprint requests may be sent to Ms. Fowler at the above address.

International Journal of Family Therapy 5(2), Summer 1983
0148-8384/83/1400-0127$02.75©1983 Human Sciences Press

and meaningful relationships. It enables members to meet certain psychological needs such as to belong, to be accepted, to release negative feelings, and to participate in self-exploration. In the positive, nurturing, yet honest and confrontive environment of the group, members can drop defenses and begin to explore threatening or troublesome aspects of life. Members who feel that their situation is unique, realize in a group setting others are facing similar circumstances. By sharing common problems, alternatives can be considered for coping more effectively with the presenting issues.

One of the strengths of the group experience is the opportunity for members to "act out" or experiment with new behavior patterns. Members may develop an awarness of inappropriate behaviors and resultant effects from such actions. When a member reverts to unsuitable behaviors, the negative response of peers is immediate. As experiences in group are translated to other situations in daily life, the individual begins to generalize responsible behavior to situations outside the group experience (Hansen et al., 1976.)

THE UTILIZATION OF GROUP

Group experiences at the Center Against Sexual Assault (CASA) are coordinated with individual counseling sessions. The four types of groups conducted on a continuous basis are: (a) Learning Lab for adults who were incest victims as children, (b) Family Forum for families of victims, (c) Offender's Group, and (d) Children's Group for child victims. There are always two, often three, facilitators for each group. These therapists are Master degree level professionals who have specialized in the treatment of incestuous families. Generally, female-male cotherapist teams are assigned to each group.

Learning Lab

The group experience for adults who were victims of sexual abuse as children is referred to as the Learning Lab. This is a carefully structured program, with 15 four-hour weekly sessions. Normally there are eight to ten clients in each group. Members are required to adhere to a written set of guidelines throughout the duration of the Lab. They are also asked at the conclusion of each week's session to write down "things I need to work on this week" and this becomes their homework assignment.

Of the individuals in the Learning Lab, 98 percent are female. The age range is from 16 to 61 with the majority, 60 percent, between 25 and 35 years of age. Clients identify substance abuse, relational problems, sexual dysfunction, depression, and low self-esteem as issues of concern to them, and attribute these difficulties directly or indirectly to the sexual abuse they suffered as children.

The 15-week program format is:

Week 1: Orientation. The therapist discusses the scheduled activities, procedures for the group, patient rights, release of information and other related information.

Week 2: Feelings. Members share why they are there, verbally recognize they were victims of sexual abuse as children, and express their feelings regarding the episodes.

Weeks 3-4: Family rules and roles. Each is asked to describe their role and the behavior of others in their families of origin.

Weeks 5-6: Destructive Behaviors. The group identifies destructive behavior patterns learned from their parents as children.

Weeks 7-8: Shame. The facilitators attempt to increase the level of openness in discussing sexual assault.

Week 9: Social hour. Group members have an opportunity to review their progress and clarify what areas to concentrate on in future sessions.

Week 10: Secrets. Members are encouraged to take risks and share the secrets of the early victimization with significant persons outside of the group.

Weeks 11-12: Sexuality. Participants discuss how their sexuality and sexual function has been affected by the sexual assault of childhood and options that are now available to them.

Week 13: New survival skills. The group lists skills learned from the family and new proficiencies acquired in the sessions.

Week 14: Finding joy. The therapists assist members in seeking help for any specific needs remaining and discuss how to exhibit responsible behavior.

Week 15: Sharing and goodbye. Each individual tells his story including what changes they have made over the past 15 weeks and where they wish to go from this point.

Aftercare is available on a situational basis; however, the clients are encouraged to be independent. A majority of Learning Lab participants are able to function without continued, regular therapy and at the conclusion of the experience report significant positive changes in their life style.

Family Forum

Family Forum is an informal weekly group for family members of the primary clients seen at the Center. It is an open entrance-exit program where people attend when they feel the need. Ninety-eight percent of the individuals in Family Forum are female. Most of them are the mothers of child incest victims.

The Family Forum experience provides an opportunity for members to problem solve in a caring environment with others in like situations. Written guidelines similar to those used in the Learning Lab are adhered to by group members. Members ask for time each week and report on homework assignments they are given. Homework assignments are situational, such as "write a letter to someone you are in conflict with and someone you appreciate," or "do something just for yourself."

Crisis issues take precedence, but everyone present has the opportunity to use the group for other purposes if they so choose. Often a specific issue will be requested as the focus of a whole session, e.g., assertiveness, dealing with anger, learning to trust, sexuality, and dealing with the criminal justice and social service systems. Many of the other topics discussed are parallel to those addressed in the Learning Lab. Relaxation and stress reduction, role play/role reversal, and guided imagery techniques are commonly used. Often in Family Forum the members form strong bonds and will informally build networks apart from the Center. This is encouraged by the staff.

Offender Group

Offender groups are limited to 12 clients and currently all members are incest offenders. Twenty-four weekly sessions are held lasting from three to four hours. Each client takes the California Psychological Inventory (1975), an attitude test (pre and post) such as the Edwards Personal Preference Schedule (1953), and completes a Sex Assessment Inventory based on the model developed by LoPiccolo and Heiman (1978). Guidelines, goal sheets, and weekly feelings sheets are similar to those employed in the Learning Lab. Currently, members of this group are all males with an average of 35.5 years. Ninety percent have high school diplomas and examples of occupations represented include police chief, minister, truck driver, college professor, construction worker, airline pilot, and engineer. Eighty percent were sexually or physically abused as children.

There are five areas that are discussed within the 24-week period. The first topic is the client's early sexual experiences in order to assess the possibility of fixation and regression as current etiological agents. The second issue is current sexuality, and developing healthy sexual relationships with adult women. Aggression, and the appropriate management of it, is the next subject discussed. The client must confront the issue of self-control and the need to channel compulsive behavior. The fourth theme is substance abuse which is often used as an excuse for behavior and to repress painful realities. Self-esteem is the last area of concern. There is always the danger that the decompensating client will deteriorate in ego functioning to borderline personality disorders. While in therapy the offender must contract not to engage in dangerous behavior, toward himself or others.

The Offender Group program is patterned after the Learning Lab. During the first several sessions, each member tells why he is there, and how he sexually offended. Participation in the group is predicated on the offender's disclosure of the sexual offense. The entry level admission may be simple acknowledgment that it is "possible" he sexually abused a child. The client is encouraged to remember details of the offense and to matriculate his behavior and responsibility. Therapeutic intervention at this point is extremely directive. The client is told that he has suppressed or repressed the details of the offending behaviors, but that he can, with concentration and cooperation, recall the particulars. It is significant to note that all the members of the offenders groups have been able to describe their past abusive behaviors.

There is one session held jointly with members of the Learning Lab, adults who were victims of sexual abuse as children. Members of each group share the reason they are participants. For example, "I am here because I sexually molested my nine-year-old daughter," or "I was sexually abused by my father from the age of two until I was sixteen." A group member may ask to work on a personal issue with the other members taking the roles of father, mother, husband, and daughter. An offender may be told by a victim how angry and hurt she feels toward all offenders. The offender in turn may be asked to apologize to his victim with one of the group members taking her role. Members of each group have the opportunity to better understand and accept one another. Few issues are taboo as topics of discussion, however, physical abuse is not permitted. Facilitating such a combined group requires sensitivity and expertise. It is not recommended for the beginning therapist or those unfamiliar with the volatile potential of this combination of clients.

In the closing sessions of the Offender Group, the members collectively process what has happened in the previous several months and individually what is the next step. Most members choose to continue working on goals set during therapy. Many will maintain their contacts with other group members and offer assistance as they move through the criminal justice system. Some will speak out publicly, e.g., on television shows, local radio talk shows, and community education programs.

The model for the Offenders' Group is still evolving. Crisis issues often occupy three to four sessions. These have included imminent court dates or incarceration, loss of job or reputation, and divorce or separation. Throughout the 24 weeks members are encouraged to assess their strengths and learn how to build self-awareness, confidence, and ultimately self-esteem.

Children's Group

The last type of group work to be discussed is the Children's Group. Groups can be as beneficial for children as they are for adults because sharing of experiences, decisionmaking in a secure environment, and knowing that one is not alone are critical for any age.

Group therapy is used as a transitional phase in moving children away from isolated, lonely, and inappropriate roles into the mainstream of childhood activity. Group therapy is not an end in itself but simply a means of facilitating the step toward peer-group integration. The child who has been sexually abused needs access to a peer group where that abuse can be revealed to other children who have suffered that same trauma, and consequently can experience bonding via the group acceptance. Many of the children seen do not have any peer resources at the time of entry.

CAROL FOWLER, SUSAN R. BURNS, JANET E. ROEHL

Three separate groups for children who have been sexually abused are conducted. They are divided according to age. Most of the children are incest victims, however children abused by people outside of the family may also be included. The preschool group is for 2 to 6 year olds, preteen includes 7 to 12 age range, and the teen group is for 13 to 18 year olds.

The preschool group numbers between 10–15 children at any given time. Activities for this group include playing house where they focus on the good things that mothers and fathers do for their children, such as singing to them or rocking them to sleep. Frequent role reversals happen in playing house so that everybody in the group gets a chance to be both parent and child. Children are encouraged to recall pleasant experiences they have had with their parents, recognize their own needs, and model toward appropriate parental behavior. Tactile play such as popping corn and baking bread is provided. Finger painting and games are used as a means for group members to interact with one another. Outings to plays and trips to petting zoos are used for healthy socialization.

The group of preteen children participate in more cognitive activities. Each member is given the opportunity to share with the group why they are there, to recognize that he or she is not the only child who has ever been sexually abused and to know that such abuse has not set them apart from other children forever. They talk about how new developments are affecting their lives, such as foster care or court appearances. Various puppets are used by this group, as are other games which facilitate the give and take of caring relationships.

The teen group is basically issue and crisis oriented. At this age adolescents are dealing with a wide range of behaviors including drug involvement, prostitution, and abusive relationships. They are coping with the integration of their sexual experiences and their sexual identity. Very frequently they request sex education. It is helpful when working with this group to remember that although they may have been sexually active for a long while that does not mean that they are sexually informed.

Role playing is used extensively in all the groups for exploration of a sundry of situations the children might have to deal with. For example, a child preparing to appear in court can be helped by being allowed to play the role of the witness and by hearing what others in the group who have already had that experience can tell them about it. A child who is being reunited with parents can play out all the positions of everyone in the family and acquire a sensitivity as to how they might react. It is reassuring for a child who is going into foster care to hear another child in the group say that while she loves her family she thinks foster care is the best place for her to be right now.

Children in both the preteen, and teen groups, keep journals. They record their thoughts and feelings in their journals and every week they give the therapist the pages they have completed the week before. These are read by the therapist, comments are made in the margins, and returned at the next group meeting. They keep all their journal pages in a folder which they bring with them to the group meetings. If the children choose to, they can share with the other members of the group something that they may have recorded in their journal.

On a week-to-week basis the groups function independently, but there are those times when they are integrated. Swim parties, weekends away, are occasions when all group members come together to enjoy companionship and participate in team efforts like volleyball and soccer. During such combined sessions, one counselor for each three children is provided. Part of the time is used for small group discussions to explore hopes for the future and long-term goals. It is expected that each small group will then come back and share what they discussed with the larger group.

All of the children's groups are unstructured so that a child who misses a session is not "left behind." This becomes important to the child who is dependent upon an adult to bring them to group. Each child is assured that they may continue to attend therapy groups for as long as they want to, and that they can tell the therapist when they do not wish to come any longer. Such an explanation reassures the children that a support line will not be cut off before they are ready.

DISCUSSION

The measure of success for any group therapy program is the individual who is able to leave the controlled group setting and establish relationships in the larger, less supervised community. CASA does not claim that the program works in every case and with every client, but the persons seen who were eventually able to mainstream, reinforces a commitment to the value of group therapy for the treatment of sexual abuse.

CAROL FOWLER, SUSAN R. BURNS, JANET E. ROEHL

REFERENCES

California psychological inventory. Palo Alto, CA: Consulting Psychologists Press, 1975.

Edward's personal preference schedule. New York: The Psychological Corp., 1953.

Hansen, J.D., Warner, R.W., and Smith, E.M. *Group Counseling: Theory and Process.* Chicago: Rand McNally College Publishing, 1976.

LoPiccolo, J., and Heiman, J.R. *Sexual assessment and history interviews.* Stony Brook, NY: State University of New York, 1978.

LoPiccolo, J., and LoPiccolo, L. (Eds.). *Handbook of sex therapy.* New York: Plenum Press, 1978.

Yamamoto, K. (Ed.) *The child and his image: Self-concept in the early years.* Boston: Houghton Mifflin Company, 1972.

Alcoholism and Incest: Improving Diagnostic Comprehensiveness

Charles P. Barnard

ABSTRACT: This article is designed to underscore the similarities in characteristics between alcoholic and incestuous family operations. Hopefully, readers will develop a more acute appreciation and understanding of the frequency of occurrence of both of these behaviors in the same family. The author contends that too often alcoholism will be diagnosed, while the incest is diagnostically missed or vice versa. To best insure that recidivism of either the alcohol or incest can be avoided, the author believes it is important to comprehensively diagnose and then treat appropriately.

One of the earliest pieces of research in the area of incest (Marcuse, 1923) identified chronic alcoholism, or a drunken episode at the least, as a primary variable in the incestuous family. Since that early work, many others have established the connection between alcoholism and incest (Herman, 1981; Justice and Justice,, 1979; Meiselman, 1978; Nedoma, Mellan, and Pondelickova, 1969; Cabinis and Phillip, 1969; Magal and Winnik, 1968; Tormes, 1968, Machotka, 1967; Cavallin, 1966; Phillip, 1966 Cormier, 1963; Szabo, 1962, Hersko, 1961; Kaufman, Peck and Tagiuri, 1954). The figures range from 15 percent of incest perpetrators, to as high as 75 to 80 percent (Meiselman, 1978; Cabinis and Philip, 1969) of all perpetrators in a particular study

Charles P. Barnard, Ed.D., is Director, Marriage and Family Therapy, University of Wisconsin-Stout, Menomonie, Wisconsin, 54751. Reprint requests may be sent to him at that address.

International Journal of Family Therapy 5(2), Summer 1983
0148-8384/83/1400-0136$02.75©1983 Human Sciences Press

group. Regardless of what the exact figure might be, it certainly seems apparent that there is a correlation between the appearance of alcoholism and incestuous practice in the family context.

My clinical experience has also verified the existence of a connection between alcoholism and incest. While it would be unrealistic to assert that all families with an adult alcoholic will be found to be incestuous, or that all incestuous families will have an alcoholic adult, it does seem safe to assume that these two behaviors will be found to coexist considerably beyond what would be expected by chance alone. Justice and Justice (1979) have identified six problems they typically address with incestuous families due to the frequency of their occurrence. These six are *alcoholism*, symbiosis, marital relationship, stress reduction, sexual climate, and isolation.

This article will identify the similarities between the "alcoholic" and "incestuous" families. The similarities seem fairly blatant, but as blatant as they are, it is unfortunate how often the alcoholism will be observed and treated, but the incest overlooked, or vice versa. One study has identified the likelihood of over 90 percent of incest cases never coming to the attention of any social agency (Gagnon, 1965). The inherent problem in treating one of these problems, but not the other, is that potential for prevention of recidivism is diminished.

As obvious as the correlation is, the "oversight" seems understandable and perhaps predictable. As professionals are trained and develop specific areas of diagnostic and treatment expertise, it is those very areas of expertise which will dictate what they most quickly diagnose and treat. Thus, the alcoholism and drug counselor will diagnose and treat drug dependency most readily, while clinicians familiar with incest will quickly diagnose and treat that behavior. It seems that as professionals, we diagnose and treat that which we know best how to diagnose and treat. Once the similarities are brought into our consciousness, and our diagnostic awareness, hopefully both phenomena can be appropriately diagnosed and treatment efforts appropriately implemented.

Lustig and his colleagues (1966) have stated the following in reference to incest in the family: "If a behavior pattern such as this (incest) reduces family tension and thus contributes to family homeostatis, it tends to become a part of that homeostatis which, once established, tends to be self-perpetuating" (pp. 32–33). While this is certainly true of incest as a regulator of a family's state of equilibrium, the same is true for alcoholism. Three recent books

(Barnard, 1981; Stanton, 1982; and Wegscheider, 1981) have firmly established this, as have numerous articles. Both incest and alcoholism have the inherent capacity to become a primary stabilizing factor in the life of a family. As the outrigger of a South Pacific canoe stabilizes and prevents the canoe from tipping, so does alcoholism/incest stabilize the family and prevent it from "tipping" and early destruction.

SIMILARITIES OF ALCOHOLIC AND INCESTUOUS FAMILIES

The following comprises a fairly representative listing of similarities between these two family dysfunctions. For purposes of this article fairly broad and generic characteristics are identified as opposed to more microcharacteristics.

1. *Blurred generational boundaries.* Justice and Justice (1979), among others, have identified the blurring of generational boundaries as characteristic of the incestuous family. Barnard (1981), Stanton (1982), and Wegscheider (1981) have identified the same generational blurring as typical of the alcoholic family. As the adult/marital relationship deteriorates, there is an increased likelihood of one of the children being "selected" to fill the role of surrogate spouse. Naturally, this can easily culminate in an incestuous relationship, and even if this is not the final outcome, this type of maneuver has detrimental effects upon both the developing child and total family operation. The blurring of these generational boundaries is what both Haley (1976) and Minuchin (1974) have identified as being inevitably linked to the development of human problems.

2. *Dysfunctional marital dyad, with a fragmented to nonexistent parental dyad.* In both of these types of families there is a problematic marital and parental dyad. Just as the existence of this phenomena can lead to the blurred generational boundaries identified above, it is similarly destructive to the total family operation. Lewis and colleagues (1976), along with Satir (1964), among others, have identified how the two adults are the "architects of the family." If their relationship is dysfunctional, there is a heightened probability that the entire family will also be troubled. The absence of a strong marital/parental relationship increases the likelihood that one of the children will become "parentified" and elevated to the status of a "pretend spouse," at least emotionally, if not sexually.

3. *Deterioration of the marital sexual relationship.* As the sexual relationship between the two adults deteriorates, the probability that incest will occur is increased. Strack and Dutton (1971) have reported from their work that nearly 100 percent of all married alcoholics report sexual dysfunctions in their marriages. As you identify greatly diminished sexual contact between mother and father, and the debilitating effect of alcohol on one's moral consciousness, the probability of incest must be considered. Similarly, the guilt and shame attached to incestuous behavior can serve to stimulate an even greater need for the numbing effect of alcohol.

4. *Normal inhibitory anxieties are short circuited or muted.* Both family types will experience the inhibition of normal anxieties which otherwise monitor the development of incestuous relationships in the family. Alcohol, as is well known, acts upon the brain in such a fashion that normal inhibitory regulators are short circuited. Similarly, in the incestuous family, normal inhibitory anxieties are muted, if not by alcohol, then through the utilization of repressive defense mechanisms. In either case, the outcome is an increased likelihood of the incestuous boundary being violated and the alcoholism and incest forming a vicious circle.

5. *Family affect is muffled and distorted.* If one considers each individual, and family, as having an "emotional keyboard," the individuals in these families only have a few keys available for "free play." These families will have difficulty with open expression of either aggression or affection, or both. It is as though these families perceive themselves as too fragile and brittle to allow expression of aggression without disintegration, or too feeble and weak to express and receive affection, out of fear of being absorbed and losing what little sense of self they do experience.

6. *Denial is rampant and "secrets" predominate.* As denial has been identified as a hallmark characteristic of the alcoholic (Jellinek, 1960), and alcoholic family (Jackson, 1954). Wegscheider, 1981), so is the same true of the incestuous family. Both family operations utilize inordinate amounts of psychic energy to maintain the "secrets" which deprive them of the potential for greater emotional expression and relatedness. As destructive as the maintenance of the secret obviously is, it is perceived by all involved as being important to preserve and maintain the delicately fragile equilibrium of the family. The activation of denial serves to further "enable" the alcoholism and incest since confrontation and intervention are avoided.

140

7. *Family roles are pathologically assigned and calcified.* As individuals are rigidly assigned roles in the alcoholic family (Barnard, 1981; Black, 1981; Wegscheider, 1981; Stanton, 1982), the same type of calcification, and resultant problems, are observed in the incestuous family. In these families there is pathological assignment of roles, with children rigidly functioning in adult roles and adults frequently appearing helpless and in need of guidance as is expected of children. The following statement by Justice and Justice about incestuous families is identical to what is observed in alcoholic families:

> When there is much role confusion, the family ceases to do the job required of a family. Children do not get limits set for them, or when limits are set, they may be arbitrary since they are being set by a child,, the sibling in power. The 'unchosen' siblings feel jealousy and resentment in seeing the 'chosen' one receive special privileges from the father (1979, p. 169).

8. *The family becomes isolated, emotionally and otherwise.* The alcoholic family isolates itself through the mechanisms of denial and erroneous problem solving. So too does the incestuous family isolate itself. Lutier (1961) has even gone so far as to suggest that isolation is the major variable associated with the evolution of incestuous relationships. The family closes itself off to outside involvement and stimulation, and begins to engage in the process of "self-suffocation." Justice and Justice have said: "One final effect of the family while the incest is going on is that the father's dependence on his daughter leads, as we noted, to his being jealous and overpossessive. His whole behavior interferes with her making normal social contacts, and the whole family becomes increasingly isolated" (1979, p. 269). As noted above, Justice and Justice indentify family isolation as one of the six problems they typically need to address with the incestuous family. The alcoholic family also insulates itself from outside involvement in order to hide the alcoholism and prevent discovery, embarrassment, shame and guilt. As these families effectively cut themselves off from outside involvement, they further seal their fate by insuring the continuation of the alcoholic and incestuous cycles. In this way the alcoholism/incest comes to be both a cause and effect of the overall family organization and operation.

9. *A profound state of pathologically rigid homeostasis or "stuckness".* The maneuvers which these families use to adapt to

the incest/alcoholism are the very mechanisms which further insure that no change will occur. As they feel more and more hopeless they engage in "more of the same" tactics which further entrenches them in the harmful consequences of the incest and alcoholism. The more denial they use, the more omnipresent the problem appears, stimulating more prominent denial, and so on. It is much like the proverbial "run-away equation" or "game without end" (Bateson, 1979).

10. *Sibling relationships come to be pathologically disturbed.* In the alcoholic and incestuous familes we observe an exceptionally high incidence of disturbed sibling relationships. In each of these families, as one child is elevated to a position of "specialness" and surrogate adult, there is an increase in confusion and frustration. As the "special child" is deprived of the opportunity to experience childhood and engage in age-appropriate activities, the other children feel deprived and "less than special." The ensuing hurt, jealousy, frustration, and inflated or deflated sense of self-esteem which is not age-appropriate, culminates in sibling relationships which are destructive to all involved.

11. *An excess of belongingness or separateness to the detriment of the other.* Minuchin (1974) has shown how individuals need to experience a sense of belongingness and a sense of separateness within their family in order to develop a functional sense of identity and self-esteem. The alcoholic and incestuous family operations provide excesses of one or the other of these important human experiences to the detriment of the other. While some family members have an excessive sense of belongingness, to the point of feeling smothered or suffocated, others experience a sense of separateness amounting to alienation with no source of functional support and nurturance. Neither of these conditions is conducive to the development of healthy, functional individuals. The consequences are shattered, partial people who have pronounced self-doubts and self-esteem problems.

12. *Intimacy and trust problems.* As parents in the alcoholic family have their sense of intimacy and trust in one another shattered, their quarrels and difficulties increase. The children observe this decompensation in their parent's conflict resolution skills and relationship. "Here the two most significant adult persons in their (children's) life are unable to solve their problems, thereby leaving the children with the generalized belief that this world must indeed be a tenuous place at best" (Barnard, 1981, p.

15). The children, like their parents, begin to have difficulty feeling comfortable enough to emotionally invest themselves in intimate relationships, generally feel an absence of trust in others, and activate various protective defense mechanisms. The same processes are in operation within the incestuous family. The incest victim feels "special," yet betrayed, while the other children feel "spared," yet unimportant. Mother and father feel unable to develop the intimacy desired in a marriage and reciprocally project blame and distance on one another as the distrust becomes pervasive. As much as these behaviors are a cause of the family dysfunction, the dysfunctional system serves to maintain these behaviors.

13. Dependency Issues. Bowen (1974) has clearly portrayed how alcoholics manifest a lack of ability to function interdependently. Stanton (1982) has similarly documented the excesses of interpersonal dependency observed in alcoholics, and how symbiosis characterizes their relationships. As alcoholics and their family relationships are characterized by dependency problems and an absence of functional and autonomous behavior, the same is true of the incestuous family. Among others, Lustig and his associates (1966) have shown how incestuous families resolve their dependency problems in non-productive ways by identifying the following as a family characteristic: "a fear of family disintegration and abandonment shared by all protagonists, such that any arrangement appears preferable to family disintegration" (Lustig, 1966, p. 39). This is also observed as a problem in the extended families as well. The parents bring unresolved dependency problems from their family of origin into the present generation, and transmit them to future generations. Perhaps one explanation for this generational transmission is found in the survival value of incest suggested by Lustig. "Thus, we propose that incest is a transaction which serves to protect and maintain a family in which it occurs. Incest can be viewed as a noninstitutionalized role relationship serving to reduce family tension by preventing confrontation with the sources of tension" (Lustig, 1966, p. 39). It seems reasonable to assume that without intervention, these same patterns of tension resolution will be transmitted to the future generations. It seems obvious that this is one source of explanation for the preponderance of alcoholism and incest being transmitted from one generation of the family to the next. In a recent book, Deutsch makes the following statement:

Three recent studies of incest and sexual abuse reported high incidences of alcohol abuse in incestuous fathers. In light of the marked tendency shown by victims of physical abuse to repeat such abuse with their own children, family alcoholism can be seen to produce not only victims but also perpetrators of this intergenerational damage. (1982, p. 7).

DISCUSSION

This article presented characteristics that are observed in both alcoholic and incestuous families. The purpose of these comparisons was to sensitize clinicians who encounter one of these problems to investigate carefully the potential presence of the other. An increase in perceptual powers should presumably result in an increase in accurate diagnosis. As Bateson has said: "Knowledge at any given moment will be a function of the thresholds of our available means of perception" (1979, p. 29). Hopefully, this article has increased "thresholds of our available means of perception" such that appropriate and thorough treatment can be brought to bear on these human problems, and much suffering alleviated.

REFERENCES

Bateson, G., Mind and Nature: A Necessary Unity. New York: E.P. Dutton, 1979.
Barnard, C.P. Families, Alcoholism and Therapy. Springfield, IL: Charles C. Thomas Publishers, 1981.
Black, Claudia. Innocent Bystanders at Risk: The Children of Alcoholics. Alcoholism: The National Magazine. 1981, 1, (3), 22–26.
Bowen, M. Family Systems Approach to Alcoholism. Addictions. 1974, 21, (2), 28–39.
Cabinis, D. and E. Phillip. Z. ges. gerichtl. med. 1969, 66, 46.
Cavallin, H. Incestuous Fathers: A Clinical Report. Amer. J. Psychiat. 1966, 122, (10), 1132.
Cormier, B.M. et al. Psychodynamics of Father-Daughter Incest. J. Can. Psychiat. Assn. 1962–163, 7, (8), 203–217.
Deutsch, D. Broken Bottles Broken Dreams. New York: Teachers College Press, 1982.
Gagnon, J. Female Child Victims of Sex Offenses. Social Problems. 1965. 13, 176–192.
Haley, J. Problem Solving Therapy. San Francisco: Jossey-Bass Pub., 1976.
Herman, J. and L. Hirschman. Families at Risk for Father-Daughter Incest. Am. J. Psychiatry. 1981, 138, (7), 967–970.
Hersko, M. et al. Incest: A Three-Way Process. J. Soc. Ther. 1961, 7, 22–31.
Jackson, J. The Adjustment of the Family to the Crisis of Alcoholism. Quarterly Journal of Studies on Alcoholism. 1954, 15, (4).
Jellineck, E.M. The Disease Concept of Alcoholism. New Haven, CT: College and University Press, 1960.
Justice, Blaire and Rita. The Broken Taboo. New York: Human Sciences Press, 1979.

Kaufman, I., A.L. Peck and C.K. Tagiuri. The Family Constellation and Overt Incestuous Relations Between Father and Daughter. *Amer. J. Orthopsychiat.* 1954, 24, 266.

Lewis, J.M. et al. *No Single Thread: Psychological Health in Family Systems.* New York: Brunner/Mazel, 1976.

Lustig, N., J. Dresser, S. Spellman and T. Murray. Incest: A Family Group Survival Pattern. *Arch. Gen. Psychiat.* 1966, 14, 31–40.

Lutier, J. Role des facteurs culturels et psycho-sociaux dans les delits incestueux en milieu rural. *Ann. Med. Leg.* 1961, 41, 80.

Machotka, P. et al. Incest as a Family Affair. *Family Process.* 1967. 6, 98–116.

Magal, V. and H.Z. Winnik. Roles of Incest in Family Structure. *Israeli Ann. Psychiat. Related Disciplines.* 1968, 6, 173–189.

Marcuse, M. Incest. *American Journal of Urology and Sexology.* 1923, 16, 273–281.

Meiselman, K.C. *Incest.* San Francisco: Jossey-Bass, 1978.

Minuchin, S. Families and Family Therapy. Cambridge, MA: Harvard University Press, 1974.

Nedoma, K., J. Mellan and J. Pondelickova. *Psychiat.* 1969, 65, 224.

Phillip, E. *Acta Med. Leg. Soc.* 1966, 19, 199.

Satir, V. *Conjoint Family Therapy.* Palo Alto, CA: Science and Behavior Books, 1964.

Stanton, M.D. and T.C. Todd. *The Family Therapy of Drug Abuse and Addiction.* New York: Guilford Press, 1982.

Strack, J.H. and L.A. Dutton. A New Approach in the Treatment of the Married Alcoholic. *Selected Papers: Twenty-Second Annual Meeting; Alcohol and Drug Problems Assoc. of America.* Hartford, CT: 1971.

Szabo, Denis. Problemes de socialixation et d'integration socioculturelles: contribution a l'etiologie de l'inceste. *Canad. Psychiat. Ass. J.*, 1962, 7, (5), 235.

Tormes, Y. *Child Victims of Incest.* Denver: The American Human Assoc.-Children's Division, 1968.

Wegscheider, S. *Another Chance.* Palo Alto, CA: Science and Behavior Books, 1981.

Incest and Professional Boundaries:
Confidentiality Versus Mandatory Reporting

Alberto C. Serrano
David W. Gunzburger

ABSTRACT: The mandatory reporting of an incest case by a mental health professional, sets in motion a chain of events which raise conflict for all involved. Typically, attorneys, the courts, health service providers, as well as primary treatment team become involved. This article discusses some of the relevant dilemmas that are raised by the personal and professional mandatory report of incest.

KEY WORDS: incest, autonomy, advocacy, intervention, clinician.

The reporting of suspected incest is a dilemma which confronts every professional in a mental health field. Although the development of laws governing the reporting of incest was altruistically motivated, clinical, medical, and social service resources are extremely limited in most communities. Hence, follow-up services frequently cannot meet the demand. Further, the complexities of treating the incestuous family are such that the theoretical confusion and clinical inadequacy can result in the treatment itself being a punishment rather than appropriate help. Finally, issues of family autonomy versus coercive intervention, (Newberger and Bourne, 1978) and compassion versus control (Rosenfeld and Newberger, 1977), as well as medical and legal am-

Alberto C. Serrano, M.D. is Clinical Professor of Psychiatry and Pediatrics and Director of Child and Adolescent Psychiatrics at the Community Guidance Center, 2135 Babcock Road, San Antonio, TX 78229. David W. Gunzburger, Ph.D. is Psychologist on the Child Abuse Team at the Center. Reprint requests may be sent to Drs. Serrano and Gunzburger at that address.

International Journal of Family Therapy 5(2), Summer 1983
0148-8384/83/1400-0145$02.75©1983 Human Sciences Press

biguities, make reporting and treatment of suspected incest a major concern for professionals.

The professional and societal dilemma is best illustrated by the family autonomy versus coercive intervention model. The traditional autonomy of the family in rearing its offspring has been recently defended by a majority of the United States Supreme Court. In a ruling against the severely beaten appellants in the controversial corporal punishment case, Ingram versus Wright, et al., a relatively new draft statute (1978–79) of the American Bar Association's Juvenile Justice Standards Project cited the poor quality of protective services in the United States and recommended to sharply restrict access to such services. They recommended, for example, to make the reporting of child neglect discretionary rather than mandatory and recommended to narrowly define the basis for court jurisdiction to situations where there is clear harm to a child. While most professionals believe this standard would make matters worse, it does speak to the realities of services following the report. It also raises the conceptual and practical problems implicit in the expansion of clinical and legal definitions of child abuse to include practically every physical and emotional risk to a child.

To the extent to which we understand that abusing parents are sad, deprived, needy human beings rather than cold and cruel criminals, we compassionately offer support and services to aid them in their struggle. However, the mandatory reporting of incest sometimes results in intervention outside of the clinical domain, including court action on the child's behalf and can result in the alienation of our patients. In practice, we are frequently forced to identify and choose the "least detrimental alternative" because the family supports which make it safe for children to live in their homes (homemakers, child care, psychiatric and medical services) are never available in sufficient amount and quality. Social/legal pressure on agencies charged with child protection frequently supports the practice of separating children from their natural homes and/or punitive action directed at the "perpetrator." The professional response of control rather than of compassion furthermore generalizes mainly to poor and socially marginal families, that is, those who appear to attract the labels "abuse and neglect" to their problems in the public setting. Affluent families avail themselves of resources more easily, demand legal counsel, etc.

ALBERTO C. SERRANO, DAVID W. GUNZBURGER

Despite the above, the reality is that as reporting and identification have become sanctioned, it has become possible to identify the "problem" as a medical issue. In reporting the perpetrator for example, we may not see him as a patient whose confidentiality has been broken, but by transforming or reframing the concept to see the family as "patients who need help." By labeling deviance as sickness, we protect our professionalism.

The legal response to child abuse was triggered by its medicalization. The perception of deviant behavior as a medical problem resulted in a call for treatment. Reporting statues codified a medical diagnosis into a legal framework. Immunity from civil liability was given to mandated reporters so long as they act in good faith. Monetary penalties for failure to report were established and familial and professional client confidentiality privileges were eliminated (except those involving attorneys). We must recognize, however, that attorneys too, feel handicapped. They must rely on the concepts that come primarily from social workers, psychologists, and psychiatrists (Newburger and Bourne, 1978). They are also torn between advocacy for their clients (most typically the parents) and advocacy for the best interest of the children. On top of all of this, incest is very difficult to characterize or to prove.

Once the report is made by a professional, the possibility of conflict of interest continues. It is not at all uncommon for an adversarial position between client and therapist to develop after the report. Without clear reading from the courts, the clinician often gets split as an advocate for one party or the other. Maintaining a family treatment model and an alliance with the family may put the clinician at odds with the legal system. Retributive aspects for the patient may also result; the medical label may protect the patient from punishment only to submit him to interminable instruction, treatment, and discrimimation which are inflicted on him for his professionally presumed benefit, i.e., psychotherapy (Illich, 1976).

With the realization that the criminal or punitive model may not protect the child, it appears that the rehabilitative ideal is in ascendance in criminal law. Still, parents may not seek help if they are fearful of prosecution. Further, even in the rehabilitative model, social distance and subordinance is inherent to the relationship between the professional and the accused. In the doctor-patient relationship, the physician is always in superordinate position because of his or her expertise. This distance necessarily increases once the label of abuser has been applied. Social distance is further exacerbated by the frequent differences between the socioeconomic status of the patient and therapist. But most importantly, once the label, "abuser" is applied, it is a very difficult one to remove and even innocent behavior is frequently viewed with suspicion. The attitude of the clinician may become that of a detective looking for deviance and pathology and making it impossible for the family to return to health.

Hence the difficulties of intervention on a purely psychiatric level do not appear without shortcoming. Further, if society defines the incestous family as sick, while there might be fewer criminal prosecutions for this problem, it is unlikely that the focus of treatment could be totally in the hands of protective services along with a variety of supportive resources. Such resources are typically in short supply. If for example, day care and competent counseling are unavailable, court action and foster placement might become the only options. The reality is that there are not enough therapists to handle all the diagnosed cases, nor do most families have the time, money, or disposition for the long-term therapeutic involvement which is absolutely necessary in so many cases. Furthermore, many lack the introspective and conceptual abilities that are required for successful psychological treatment. Most of us prefer to avoid coercion and punishment and to keep families autonomous and services voluntary. We must acknowledge, however, the realities of family life and recognize that the legal role is necessary to assure the well-being of children.

Physicians need to be more aware of the complexity of human life, especially in social and psychological dimensions. Attorneys might be helped to learn that in child custody cases for example, they are not merely advocates for a particular position. The medical, psychological, or social work clinician needs to be aware too, of the above mentioned issues, their effects on his/her ability to treat the patient, and the fact that in either a direct or indirect way, treatment of these individuals is a mandate from the community.

It is clear that despite the obvious coercive aspects of the clinical involvement, a direct, honest, and straightforward presentation of our role as healing/supporting agents rather than persecutors or detectives often goes a long way. Most of the families of incest have lived with these "secrets" long enough to have problems trusting openness and honesty. Experience and research suggest serious familial dysfunction, and frequent equally serious individual dysfunction in these patients. Conflicts are often pre-oedipal and treatment is often long, with rehabilitation being a difficult and rocky process. As clinicians, we often have a consider-able amount of power in the courts as expert witnesses. Our clinical opinions weigh considerably in the future of these families return to some form of integrity or the possible loss of a child and the threat of a jail sentence. While treatment under the pressure of legal mandate is less desirable and often less effective than voluntary participation in treatment, it is by no means unreward-ing. No doubt many clinicians, find this work stressing, experienc-ing anger or depression in response to familial resistance and to legal or clinical complications. However, by viewing ourselves as the patient's advocate, we can decrease our own stresses and hopefully decrease the adversarial dimensions of at least the patient-clinician relationship.

REFERENCES

Illich, I. Medical nemesis: The exploration of health. New York: Random House, 1976.
Ingram V. Wright. 4 SLW 4364 U.S. Supreme Court, 1977.
Newberger, E. H., and Bourne, R. The medicalization of child abuse. In J. Eekear and S. Katz (Eds.), Family Violence. Toronto: Butterworths, 1978.
Rosenfeld, A. and Newberger, E. Compassion vs control: Conceptual and practical pitfalls in the broadened definition of child abuse. Journal of the American Medical Association, 1977, 237, 2086–2088.

MOVING? ———————— SUBSCRIBING?

Title of Journal: _____

Please check:
☐ I have moved and have listed my old and new address below.
☐ I would like to subscribe. **SEE FRONT OF ISSUE FOR PRICES.**
    ☐ **Check enclosed**

    ☐ **Charge my credit card**
       ☐ Visa;   ☐ Master Charge;   ☐ American Express
       Card No.:_____

Old Address: Name _____
            Affiliation _____
            Address _____
            City, State, Zip _____

New Address:
Name _____
Affiliation _____ **HUMAN SCIENCES PRESS, INC.**
Address _____ **72 FIFTH AVENUE,**
City, State, Zip _____ **NEW YORK, N.Y. 10011**

Wise, Jonathan Kurland, M.D.
and Susan Kierr Wise

THE
OVEREATERS

Eating Styles
and Personality

How to lose excess weight is a national obsession. Yet despite the numerous highly publicized remedies which have been suggested for this problem, millions of Americans cannot control overeating and are seemingly impervious to help. Clearly a new approach is needed—and this book is a significant answer to that need.

Unlike other works in the field, *The Overeaters* examines the complexity of the problem, rather than reducing it to a few simple *do's* and *dont's*. The widely varying causes of overeating are approached through a system of classification which relates specific eating disorders to their sources in major stages of psychic and sexual development.

. . . It presents some illuminating insights into the psychological and medical reasons for being overweight. Case histories illustrate problems, treatment and results . . . provides an unusual depth of information and understanding"
—Library Journal

"This book informs with understandable medicine and sensible psychotherapy. In addition to excellent discussions of custom and psychodynamics, the authors clearly explain treatment strategies and include an outstanding discussion of the use of supervised body movement to unlock frozen eating scripts."
—Houston Chronicle

". . . the Wises offer tools for diagnosing your particular styles of eating, and ways of changing it for the better. You'll get everything from a serious medical view of the overeater to fat personality profiles. The writing . . . is studded with good stories from real life and much insight." —Family Health

1979   224 pp.   LC 79-719
0-87705-405-3

HUMAN SCIENCES PRESS, INC.
72 FIFTH AVENUE,
NEW YORK, N.Y. 10011